42 Rules of Social Media for Small Business

By Jennifer L. Jacobson
Foreword by Jory Des Jardins

E-mail: info@superstarpress.com
20660 Stevens Creek Blvd., Suite 210
Cupertino, CA 95014

Copyright © 2009 by Jennifer L. Jacobson

All rights reserved. No patent liability is assumed with respect to the use of the information contained herein. Although every precaution has been taken in the preparation of this book, the publisher and author assume no responsibility for errors or omissions. Neither is any liability assumed for damages resulting from the use of the information contained herein.

First Printing: October 2009
Paperback ISBN: 978-1-60773-014-9 (1-60773-014-6)
Place of Publication: Silicon Valley, California, USA
Library of Congress Number: 2009933219

eBook ISBN: 978-1-60773-015-6 (1-60773-015-4)

Trademarks

All terms mentioned in this book that are known to be trademarks or service marks have been appropriately capitalized. Super Star Press™ cannot attest to the accuracy of this information. Use of a term in this book should not be regarded as affecting the validity of any trademark or service mark.

Warning and Disclaimer

Every effort has been made to make this book as complete and as accurate as possible, but no warranty of fitness is implied. The information provided is on an "as is" basis. The author, contributors, and publisher shall have neither liability nor responsibility to any person or entity with respect to any loss or damages arising from the information contained in the book.

If you do not wish to be bound by the above, you may return this book to the publisher for a full refund.

Praise For This Book!

"A solid perspective—based on over a decade of history, clear writing, and tons of real-world examples—makes '42 Rules of Social Media for Small Business' a strong introduction for marketers and entrepreneurs looking to grow their business through social media."
Shel Horowitz, Social Media Consultant and Award-winning Author of six marketing books, http://www.frugalmarketing.com

"Jennifer Jacobson shows how easy it is to step into the virtual cocktail party of social media with her '42 Rules of Social Media for Small Business.' This book comes at a perfect time when business owners are discovering that conversations are being had about them online."
Dave Saunders, davesaunders.net

"It seems that every day I meet a small businessperson who has never experienced social media firsthand. They don't understand what social media can do, how it works or where they should start. Now entrepreneurs can start by reading this book. '42 Rules of Social Media for Small Business' is full of anecdotes, insights and advice that are sure to get an entrepreneur on their way towards leveraging social networks as part of their overall marketing strategy. It's a good read and one that I will be recommending frequently."
Erik Wolf, President of Zero-g Creative and Gravity Free Radio Show Host

"If you're a small business looking to implement a social media strategy, consider Jennifer Jacobson's '42 Rules of Social Media for Small Business' as your bible. This comprehensive book addresses the questions and concerns most often posed by businesses that are seeking to understand this new form of conversation. Using time-tested marketing concepts, concise explanations and practical examples, this book focuses on the components and best practices for a successful social media strategy. In the fast-changing world of online communication, '42 Rules of Social Media for Small Business' is sure to stand the test of time. I will be recommending this book as a 'must-read' to my small business clients."
Marlene Gavens, Owner, The Savvy Seller

"Getting the swing of social media is a big deal for small businesses. But there are some rules to this online playground, and Jacobson's new book nails them."
Jane Mascarella, Freelance Journalist and Editorial Director of The Long Island Exchange

"'42 Rules of Social Media for Small Business' is impressively researched, beautifully illustrated and thoughtfully written. It is a must read for every professional and individual, be it in making of 'Large or Small Business.' This book will be an enriching and self-encouraging experience and will help entrepreneurs to 'Think Out of the Box.'"
Sandeep Gupta, Head Business Development, Universal Medicare Pvt. Ltd.

Epigraph

"If you are in this business, and you're about communicating, you need to understand what millions of people are doing online. You should create yourself a Facebook page, a MySpace page, or something of the like, because you need to get it if you're going to help communicate and be part of what I call a digital revolution."[1]
Patrick Walker, Head of Video Partnerships, Google
At *Communicating the Museum* Conference, 2008

"Many small businesses nowadays are taking advantage of social media because it is incredibly efficient and portable. You can do it from your phone, your laptop, and just about anywhere. I have interviewed many local businesses owners who use social media and they all have one thing in common, they all use social media to communicate valuable messages to their specific target audiences."
Scott Budman of NBC 11's *Tech Now* in an exclusive conversation at the 2009 140 Twitter Conference

"The basic tool for the manipulation of reality is the manipulation of words. If you can control the meaning of words, you can control the people who must use the words."[2]
Philip K. Dick
'How to Build a Universe That Doesn't Fall Apart Two Days Later'

Dedication

For Adam, without whose brilliance I would not have finished this book and also for Pepper the Wonder Dog, who slept at my feet through every chapter and diligently reminded me to take breaks so we could play ball.

Acknowledgments

Social media is a hot button topic and an effective, affordable way for small businesses to compete in today's market. I would like to thank everyone who contributed and offered to contribute to this book. I would especially like to thank Laura Lowell for helping me through the writing process and Jory Des Jardins for contributing the foreword. Thank you to Scott Budman of Tech Now, Alex Payne of Twitter, Lauren Elliott of PNN, Kristen Nicole of Mashable, and Jim Griffith of eBay. A special thank you to Peter Shankman for HARO (Help a Reporter Out). And of course, thank you to everyone who reads this book and finds it helpful. '42 Rules of Social Media for Small Business' is filled with stories and advice from real-world social media experts who have learned how to make social media work for them. Their enthusiasm helped make this book the survival guide I hoped it would be.

Contents

Foreword	Foreword by Jory Des Jardins 1
Intro	The Changing Context Of Communication. 5
Rule 1	Rules Are Meant To Be Broken. 8
Part I	Social Media Communication 101. 10
Rule 2	Communication Is Communication Both On And Offline 12
Rule 3	Know Your Audience. 14
Rule 4	Thoughtful Social Media Generates Thoughtful People 16
Rule 5	You Don't Need a Million Friends 18
Rule 6	People Only Blog If They Think Someone Is Listening 20
Rule 7	If You Write a Good Blog, People Will Read It 22
Rule 8	People Recognize Bad Viral Behavior 24
Rule 9	When 1 Person Complains, 100 Support You, And 500 Don't Even Notice. 26
Rule 10	Not Everyone Follows The Rules 28
Rule 11	There's Always a Reason To Communicate 30
Part II	Your Business's Identity 32
Rule 12	Build a Great Profile. 34

Rule 13	Not Everyone Needs a MySpace Page	 36
Rule 14	Meet With Customers Virtually	 38
Rule 15	Use Your Own Media	 40
Rule 16	Have a Username That Reflects Your Business	 42
Rule 17	Build a Virtual Home	 44
Rule 18	Get a Real Email Address	 46
Rule 19	Edit Your Media	 48
Part III	Understanding Social Media	 50
Rule 20	Know Your Social Media Platforms	 52
Rule 21	Learn To Evolve With Technology	 54
Rule 22	Find Social Media Platforms That Work For You	 56
Rule 23	Eighteen-Year-Olds Will Always Be Ahead Of You In Technology	 58
Rule 24	Your Social Media Page Is Not Your Website	 60
Rule 25	Engage Customers First. Then Sell.	 62
Rule 26	Have Enough Lifeboats To Save Your Blog	 64
Rule 27	Real Customers Are More Than Friends	... 66
Part IV	Mastering Your Skills	 68
Rule 28	Be Findable	 70
Rule 29	Flaunt It With a Podcast	 72
Rule 30	Link Like There's No Tomorrow	 74

Rule 31	Spoon Feed The Press.	76
Rule 32	Friends Don't Let Friends Pay Full Price	78
Rule 33	Get a Guru.	80
Rule 34	Blog Your Best Blog	82
Rule 35	A Little Planning Goes a Long Way	84
Rule 36	Publicize Your Company Events	86
Rule 37	Make a Killer Virtual Portfolio	88
Rule 38	It's All Fun And Games Until They Find Out What You Did Last Summer.	90
Rule 39	Kevin Bacon Is Your Friend	92
Rule 40	Maximize Online Directories	94
Rule 41	Advertise With Social Media	96
Rule 42	These Are My Rules. What Are Yours?	98
Appendix A	Resources And References.	100
Author	About the Author.	102
Your Rules	Write Your Own Rules	104
Books	Other Happy About Books	106

Foreword

Foreword by Jory Des Jardins

Congratulations on taking the first step and acknowledging that the world is changing, for the better.

Ten years ago—heck, even five years ago—you did not have tools of influence at your disposal like you do today. It's an empowering, and intimidating thought. Anyone who starts a small business now has the ability to generate thought leadership—and customers—any place in the world that has a Web connection. This fact also makes true a new reality: A lot of digital clutter exists in the world and, without a smart, actionable way to take advantage of these tools (and a lot of patience and hard work) you won't rise to the top of Google searches, get indexed on lists of top blogs, or attract immediate responses to your Tweets. Your efforts, like most of the poorly executed online campaigns, won't be seen.

But this isn't an either/or proposition. Even people who don't have ten hours a day to spend online (I acknowledge that people who aren't in digital media might not) can build businesses from engaging in social media. Not all of us are trying to be blogebrities or have the most friends on MySpace; many of us are just trying to grow a business. I can accept that some of you simply want to leverage these tools, but don't blame me or Jennifer, if in the process you become obsessed with them.

You see, once you begin to actively engage in social media you find that making connections for yourself and for others becomes a way of doing business. A close friend asked me, three years ago, how she could change careers through blogging. Before setting her up with a blog account, I suggested she read blogs of natural interest, perhaps even comment on a few. She did that, and began making connections with others in her field. Soon, when she determined she was ready to launch her own blog, she had a built-in audience of followers who read her posts about people making a difference for non-profits. At this point she wasn't running a business but a well-positioned dialogue that listed her prominently in Web searches around tech and non-profits (a nice little side benefit of engaging in blogging). Today she runs a consulting business for non-profits seeking viable online marketing programs. Her podcasts are featured on iTunes and she's constantly approached with new consulting projects. Blogging has given her income, options, and a flexible lifestyle.

Others need to cultivate customer communities, like the online shoe retailer, Zappos, whose CEO has developed a legendary status for his approachability on Twitter, or attract a niche base, like Sarah Endline, whose blog, Sweetriot, has made a name for her free-trade chocolate business. Some leverage social media to re-establish relationships, like Dell did for its small business customers by creating a Facebook page with useful tools and resources. Dell isn't a small business, but it approached social media like one-starting small, and attracting the right people to its page. Some, like Canadian small business Mabel's Labels, amplified their low-budget marketing initiatives by announcing them on Twitter. In early 2009, the brand offered a free ticket to a popular conference for women bloggers (one that my organization, BlogHer, produces). Women immediately responded on Twitter by telling their audiences about the giveaway and encouraging their blogging peers to enter the contest by posting about what inspires them to blog. Mabel's Labels earned 2,355 blog mentions and, according to site tracker Alexa, more than tripled its page views from the best month the corporate site had all of the previous year.

All of these businesses used social media, and none of these initiatives happened overnight. They began with a decision to embrace social media tools and a commitment to use them well. Like with anything powerful, there are misuses, downright abuses, and failures. This isn't a medium to be taken lightly. When you aren't thoughtful, the end user remembers, and the Web refuses to let you forget. What seemed like a harmless picture posted of you enjoying an NRA rally on Flickr could come back to haunt you. If there's anything you take away from Jennifer's book, it's that you must take the time to understand not only the technology, but also the implications of using it.

Once you have taken this time, there's nothing to be afraid of, except maybe for the breakdown of your server from an onslaught of a million customers immediately seeking your services.

...But let's not get ahead of ourselves.

Jory Des Jardins,
Co-Founder of BlogHer

Intro

The Changing Context Of Communication

History has seen the opening and closing of many frontiers. John Ford's films document the closing of the Old West. The 'Little House on the Prairie' book series documents the same closing, from a more personal perspective. Even my own grandmother has stories from her Oklahoma childhood—about riding her horse at night, only to hear the chanting of Native American tribes drifting on the wind from miles away. After the spoken language, humankind invented ways in which to write and send messages. We created (to name a few) written histories, the Library of Alexandria, the telegraph, the telephone, the radio, the television, the computer, and the internet. With each new technological medium for advancing communication, humankind has invented new rules and structures. And as our capacity to communicate across new technologies grew, humankind has seen new worlds, and cultivated and occupied those new worlds until our gaze reached beyond the next horizon, beyond the next ocean, and up to the moon, and stars.

I grew up within a strong small business economy in the nurturing light of California's Silicon Valley. At that time, the possibilities for rapid growth and unforeseen wealth loomed in front of the local economy like a golden specter and Silicon Valley was affectionately referred to as the new Wild West. Today however, we are witnessing the closing of a great virtual frontier. With the dotcom gold rush and subsequent bust behind us and the rise and plateau of new and social media, many businesses are wondering if they missed something; if it's too late. Others are still asking the question; *what is social media?*

This book has been written to give small businesses a long-term perspective on digital communication, because in my experience, a long-term perspective is essential to the survival of any business, organization, or idea. For this reason, '42 Rules of Social Media for Small Business' is not filled with wiz-bang, techno jabber that is prone to constant change. It is, however, filled with the principles of online communication as well as guideposts around what to do, what not to do, and why. Frontiers evolve. Technology changes. A hot, trendy social media hub today might be old hat six months from now. Ideas that are well conveyed, however, do not expire. Small businesses don't have an unlimited amount of time to constantly research and test new social media sites. They do, however, have time to do their homework, select a few social media platforms, stick with them, and make an impact. The small businesses that learn to adapt quickly to the ever-changing landscape of technology will better position themselves for success and long-term survival.

Social media is affecting the ways in which people communicate, both on a personal and global scale. Chris Hughes, co-founder of Facebook and coordinator of the Obama campaign's social networking site[3] (http://www.mybarackobama.com), champions the individuals behind social media technology. "What has made My.BarackObama unique hasn't been the technology itself, but the people who used the online tools to coordinate offline action," Chris wrote in his blog in November of 2008.[4] "My.BarackObama has always been focused on using online tools to make real-world connections between people who are hungry to change our politics in this country." For small businesses, the ability to involve your target audience online can mean the difference between success and failure. It is with high hopes that I encourage you to learn from this book, the rules of communication in this wonderfully changing frontier.

Rule 1

Rules Are Meant To Be Broken

You don't need to know everything there is to know about social media to make it work for you.

In May of 1996, unsuspecting Vermont resident Jim Griffith was online, looking to upgrade memory in his old IBM PS/2 computer, when he ran across, and fell in love with a website he had never used before—eBay. In no time at all, Jim, or "Griff" as he likes to be known, found himself spending upwards of 90 hours a week fielding eBay customer questions on a gratis basis. In a sense Griff was breaking the rules—he was spending extensive amounts of his own time working for free, in a marketplace that wasn't very well known. But working hard at something you love has its ways of paying off. By mid summer of 1996, eBay's founder, Pierre Omidyar, and his business partner, Jeff Skoll, invited Griff to join eBay as their first Customer Support Representative. Today, Griff is the official "Dean of eBay Education" and serves as a spokesperson, ambassador, and weekly radio show host with "eBay Radio" and "Ask Griff." So, while some say it's important to play by the rules and do things by the book, in many ways, life is all about following what you love and breaking the rules.

While it may seem counter intuitive to start a "rule book" with a rule about breaking rules, remember that it is the rule breakers who make history. These are the people who push the envelope, who ask "why," who listen to their own curiosities, and make their own observations.

There is a fascinating BBC series called *Connections*. Started in the seventies, the series explained how a rubber band is connected to digital computing and how the concept of the vacuum is connected to the atom bomb. James Burke, the science historian who hosted the show, poses the fundamental problem with the nature of his profession: "By the time you have learned something, it is already obsolete." I believe it is not too far of a stretch to say that by the time you have learned all you can about social media, and by the time you fully understand how to put it into practice, what you have learned will be obsolete.

This is the fundamental problem of the dog chasing its tail. The tail is always in front of the dog, and always behind the dog. So what is the secret to social media success with business? How do you learn all you can about your child, before she becomes an adult? How do you try to look younger, while every year, growing undeniably older? This question is one that is at the heart of existence.

Perhaps the question itself is flawed. For social networking I offer an elegant, simple solution that transcends the question, and in bypassing the initial question, I too am breaking a rule. It is not about learning everything there is to know about social media. Social media is like any other social situation. It's all about exposing yourself, getting into new situations, learning new things, and adapting to new circumstances. Social media is meant to be used and explored. Explore the world of social media as it appears to you. Visit new sites, take notes, learn about your virtual surroundings, and remember, there is no one right way to do it. You don't need to know everything there is to know about social media to make it work for you. You just need to know enough and if you can learn a little extra you'll be better off for it.

So while you learn about how to apply the rules in this book to your social media for business efforts, I encourage you to learn to think for yourself. Remember that you are a member of the human species that is constantly learning and discovering. Apply your new learning while you stay very much in tune with who you are and confident in what your business does for the world.

Part I
Social Media Communication 101

Just getting started in social media? Learn the fundamentals of social media communication—why to communicate and who to communicate with.

Rule 2

Communication Is Communication Both On And Offline

Customers appreciate genuine online communication as much as they do a sincere handshake and a smile.

If you have recently discovered social media and feel confused, this is perfectly normal. The mass that is you and your social media presence is miniscule compared to the vast realm of space. The amount of time you exist on this planet, (and the amount of time the planet exists) is so incredibly small compared with the timeline of the rest of the universe, that doing anything may seem futile. However, it is at this point of the story that I like to fall back on an idea, which I hope will illuminate your personal path to social media enlightenment, as well as enlightenment in general. The idea is this: *The meaning of life is for life to have meaning.*

Now ask yourself, "Why am I here?" You will find that you are not alone. Some ask this question while waiting in line at the grocery store, others ask it while watching the horizon as a storm approaches, and still others, late at night, while staring at a glowing computer screen. To this, I offer the idea that life is a series of events in which you find yourself, and in which you find others. The flip side also exists; a series of events in which you let go of yourself and in which you let go of others.

I suggest, and I am not the first to do so, that we can do two profound things with our lives—listen and communicate. It is okay to listen, to be still, and listen. It is okay to create, and it can be wonderful to have relationships. Technology changes, but the human desire to listen and communicate remains. So, if you have come this far, then you are ready to venture into the rabbit hole that is social media because communication is communication, whether it happens through a social media platform, or through face-to-face interaction between individuals.

Kristen Nicole was a budding writer who would have had a rather sheltered childhood were it not for the online social networks she communicated through. AOL chat rooms, BlackPlanet, Friendster, MySpace, Facebook, and Twitter kept her in contact with her firends. Even when Kristen studied Biopsychology at the University of Michigan, she remained active in these networks because they enabled her to keep in contact with her friends in the undergraduate program. Kristen used social media to stay connected much in the same way people used to do with letters, phone calls, face-to-face visits, and even emails. While you may know Kristen today from Mashable.com, where she was their first employee and head writer, and also as the author of 'The Twitter Survival Guide,' there was a time when Kristen was new to social networks and social media. "Be genuine in building your networks," Kristen advises. "Otherwise customers will be turned off. Join the conversation—don't dominate it or impose yourself into it." The level of honesty that Kristen suggests is essential to effective online communication. "Use real names, real people from your business and engage others for personal as well as professional reasons."

Social media platforms are like a galaxy; every day we learn a little more about it, and every day it moves a little further away. Social media is, at its core, social. Online communication comes with rules, lessons, and messages just like face-to-face communication does. The key to effective online communication is to understand the signals you send and receive. Apply what you know about face-to-face communication to your online practices. You are, after all, representing yourself and your business, so communicate through social media to your customers with the same mindset you have when you see them in person. Virtual customers appreciate genuine online communication as much as they do a sincere handshake and smile.

Rule 3

Know Your Audience

You can't speak personally to someone if you have no idea who they are.

One of the hallmarks of a good business social media campaign is your ability to speak to your audience in a way that encourages them to do business with you. While there is a multitude of tips, tricks, and techniques for communicating online, in a social environment, none of them work well if you don't know exactly who you are talking to.

Unlike broadcast media, social media is very personal and something that everyone can engage in and interact with. In order to maintain that personal touch with your social media campaign, you have to know your audience and speak to them at their level and in their terms. Imagine you are giving a presentation about what you do at work, for your second grader's "bring your parent to school day." You would, ideally, dress appropriately, and discuss what you do at work on a level the children can understand. You might even bring pictures and a video presentation to help them relate to your job and why it is an important part of the community. You would know that talking above them would lose their interest, while baby-talking to them would offend their intelligence.

The same is true with social media. You have to know exactly where your audience is. You should know the profile of your ideal customer and it should include very specific points that are relevant to your company and product. What age group are they in? What is their average annual household income? What television, radio, or webcasts do they consume? How do they get their news? What do they like most about your brand?

"It's important for businesses to know who their audiences are because businesses are about satisfying the wants and needs of customers, and that's hard to do without a thorough understanding of who those customers are," says John Martin, Founder and CEO of Crowd Science. In 2006, after leaving ComScore, John began thinking about the need for businesses to know their audiences. While panel research, like that offered by Nielsen, was available, it was also very expensive and not always representative of a business's exact audience. Eventually John, with the help of Paul Neto and John Wainwright, created Crowd Science, a demographics platform that provides businesses with real time audience demographics at an affordable price point. "There is value in gaining an understanding of your audience and it needs to have some level of statistical reliability," John admits. "There is no need to go overboard, but the use of simple, well-known research tools and techniques can turn an assumption about your customers into a fact. And facts go a lot further in growing your business than assumptions."

While large corporations often spend hundreds of thousands of dollars on research, you can use modern technology to get to know your audience at a price point that suits your budget. To drill down to the specifics about your audience you should consider using a demographics query on your website and your social media platforms, like that offered by Crowd Science Demographics, PollDaddy, or SurveyMonkey. Remember to keep your surveys short and simple. Only ask the questions that you need answers to, and be sure to provide enough options in the multiple-choice answers.

Surveys enable you to know your audience in an instant, letting you track changes in buyer preferences and update your product lines appropriately. The more information you have on what your customers really want and need, the better informed you'll be when it comes to delivering something they are likely to buy.

Rule 4

Thoughtful Social Media Generates Thoughtful People

If you want people to see your social media and interact with you, you have to give them something in return.

Blogs, emails, and your social networking pages are more than ways to update your customers on new products or services. They are vessels that create community around your company. Think of the Walt Disney Company. What started as a cartoon mouse evolved into a cast of characters, the Mickey Mouse Club, feature-length cartoons, educational films, Disneyland, Epcot Center, the Disney Channel, Disney Family.com, several online ventures, and one of the largest empires known to modern communications. Companies like Disney, Apple, Google, Volvo, and McDonald's, to name a few, don't just tell customers about their new products and services. They create a community, a cult even, that spreads the word for them.

Mac Rumors spreads stories about speculated Apple upgrades, products, and services. Google releases "beta" versions of its products that become cool, must-have programs, long before the media ever knows about them. Disney markets many of their products to children, who are never without the most current information regarding Hannah Montana, or Winnie the Pooh.

When Lauren Elliott, co-creator of the Brøderbund game *Where in the World is Carmen Sandiego?* set out to make a Web publishing platform he knew he wanted a place that was simple enough for first-timebloggers to actively share and engage with very little knowledge of the technology behind the platform. Years prior, having gone through the difficult process of publishing a book, which focused on his well-known mother, niece to Eleanor Roosevelt, Lauren was familiar with the difficulties commonly facing would-be writers. Publishing a physical book was time-consuming and difficult, and publishing online was often too hard for people not born with a computer mouse in hand. Yet Lauren knew there were stories in the world from everyday people, and he wanted to collect and distribute them.

When Lauren introduced PNN (The Personal News Network) to the public in 2007, he quickly found that the people using his online publishing platform appreciated its usability and that they were generating heartfelt, thoughtful content. As PNN grew, its authors' well-written stories and media attracted a loyal, thoughtful following. "In order for someone to share and interact in a social media space, they have to feel comfortable and safe in the virtual environment," says Lauren. "Not all social media platforms work for every type of person. If you want people to read your blog and interact with you, you have to give them something in return. You have to be honest and direct and able to share."

Your social media campaigns need to be thoughtful, well-crafted tools that promote:
- Industry and Product Education
- Urgency
- Interactivity
- Loyalty

How to involve customers in your online campaigns:
- Make a unique, attractive-looking social media site
- Make sure your site is easy to use and interact with
- Ask customers industry-related questions about what they want
- Leave room for feedback and be easy to contact
- Ask for customer input when appropriate
- Post success stories from your customers
- Start a "Customer of the Month" club

Your social media space is your little part of the world to create your own "My Company Land." Creating this type of an environment, a good product, and the buzz to accommodate it, invites customers to be excited and proactive about your company. Letting them discover the benefits of your product and teaching them will go a lot farther than pounding them over the head with product benefits and messaging. Remember, customers like to feel like they've accomplished something. Give them a place to discover your business and fall in love with your product, and you're on your way to building a company that does more than sell a product, you sell an idea—the idea that life is better when customers choose you.

Rule 5

You Don't Need a Million Friends

Connect with businesses and companies that you know and let your network grow organically.

Defining your goals is an important part of any business campaign, whether online or offline. It is important to define your social media goals and ask yourself if you want millions of online followers, or a select group of online friends who will gladly do business with you. While having millions of friends on your Facebook page or millions of followers on Twitter may sound appealing, it's not always a realistic goal, and it may even be counterproductive to your business's social media efforts.

Imagine you won the lottery and you could have any amount of cash you desired. How much money would you ask for? Chances are you'd want millions, possibly billions, of dollars. Considering the government bailouts that have recently been circulated, you might even ask for trillions. In reality, what we claim to want and what we would be comfortable with can be two very different things.

Let's take a look at what can happen when we get what we wish for. An individual given millions of dollars suddenly has a new set of concerns and questions. Who will inherit the money when they die? How will they spend their money? Will they donate any of it to charity? How will they keep their money safe? Do people like them because they are rich or do they like them because of who they are? Sometimes, as many good stories teach, getting what you wish for isn't really in your best interest.

Social media is very much the same; while many people say they want a million friends, it wouldn't meet their business needs or goals. First of all, if all of these friends decided to visit your company's website, could your servers handle a million hits? Second, real friendships are more than a shout out. People who are the most valuable to your business's social media efforts are actively communicating, commenting, posting pictures, and videos, and learning about your product with the intent of doing business with you either now or in the future. Do you have the capacity to communicate with a million people like this?

Take, for example, these thoughts on the importance of strategically socializing, as opposed to the spray and pray spam method. Susan Gunelis, President and CEO of KeySplash Creative, Inc. says, "Social media is the key to brand-building these days. People are online and it's the perfect place to connect with them. More people are influenced by blogs and online relationships than by traditional media."

"My favorite social media story comes from Universal Studios in Orlando, Florida," Susan says. "In 2007, with a virtually limitless budget, the marketing exec at Universal was tasked with announcing and promoting the new Harry Potter theme park that would open in the coming years. To spread the word, she didn't turn to traditional advertising. At the risk of being fired for her out-of-the-box approach, she announced a webcast to just seven people who were also popular Harry Potter bloggers. The webcast required a password that only those seven people had. During the webcast, she revealed the news of the upcoming Harry Potter theme park and, within twenty-four hours, there were hundreds of thousands of Web searches for the Harry Potter theme park. From zero to nearly one million people within twenty-four hours. Now that's the power of social media!"

Your social media efforts will be much more effective if you set goals. Unless you're selling ad space on your social media page, it doesn't matter if you have a million friends. It just matters that you have the right friends; friends who will promote your brand, and do business with you. For most small businesses, it is better and more realistic to maintain the friends they have and look for qualified potential social media friends. Try to connect with businesses and companies that you have done business with and let your network grow from there.

Rule 6

People Only Blog If They Think Someone Is Listening

Imagine who your social media audience is and speak to them directly.

Have you ever been at the front of a board room, giving a presentation on your team's progress, excitedly pointing out trends of productivity and forecasting next quarter's growth, only to find the people at the board room table staring back at you blankly—uninterested and disengaged? You'd probably think, 'How dare they! I'm up here giving my presentation that I prepped for and practiced, and all they can do is text on their cell phones and ignore my efforts.' And you'd be right. If you don't think anyone is listening to you, you're less likely to try to communicate.

Social media creators are much the same way. People try to communicate only if they think there is a good chance someone will listen. Unfortunately, we've all experienced the letdown of not being listened to, whether on the phone with a customer service representative, in a store while trying to return a product, and sometimes, even by our own friends and family. Not being listened to detours us from wanting to continue attempted communication with a group or individual. As a business, it is important to listen to your customers, and while many business owners know how to listen, they sometimes get lost on the finer points of sending out the correct messages about their business.

For this reason, a blog or a tweet can be a very scary thing for businesses new to social media. An entire blank slate stares at them from their computer screen, and they have no idea how to use it or what to say.

Recently, I spoke with Alex Payne, Twitter's API Lead at the 140 Twitter Conference in Mountain View, California, and he suggested that businesses communicate what their customers want to hear. "The value of Twitter for your business is that it enables you to connect with customers on an ongoing basis," Payne said. "If you have a diner you can tweet your daily special. If you have a hardware store, you can tweet your spring-cleaning promotion. Success on Twitter is not about tweeting at people. Success on Twitter is about making the time and having the motivation to tweet with people, and answer their questions."

Remember to do your homework:

- **Look Around You:** Read other blogs, tweets, and social media posts in your industry.
- **Investigate:** Ask your customers what social media platforms they belong to.
- **Don't Write Live:** Write practice blog entries of your own and save them as a text document (this way they won't accidentally get published prematurely).
- **Visualize Your Reader:** While writing your blog entry, imagine your reader, your customer—the person listening to you.
- **Test Drive It:** Try reading your blog entry aloud as if your reader is sitting in the chair next to you. If possible, read the blog entry to one of your customers and see if it attracts their interest.
- **Get Feedback:** Ask for your customer's feedback and take it into account. If they say they liked the story you told about your first sales pitch, add personal stories to your blog. If they say they liked the inside tips you gave on how to fix a leaky sink, include more do-it-yourself home repair tips in your blog.

Remember, your audience is listening to you. Use your blog to educate them in an area that complements your business. Share your stories. Make it personal. A personal, informed touch is the hallmark of a good blog and while it may take a while to find your voice in your blog, you'll find it gets easier the more you realize your audience is actually interested in what you have to say.

Rule 7

If You Write a Good Blog, People Will Read It

The average blog has one reader. To survive, you have to be above average.

When was the last time you had a full conversation with yourself? If you're like most people, you probably don't do it often, if ever. When you have something to say, you find a way to communicate it with others. After all, humans developed the ability to speak out of the need to communicate something beyond grunts and squeals. Today people use many methods to communicate, and one of them is through the online communication platform known as the blog. Blogs are intended to be read, and as such, their writers usually write with the intention of their work being read.

When you write your company's blog, keep in mind that, if it is good, well tagged, and easy to find, people will read it. While this may seem obvious, I have seen actual blog posts from business owners who seemed to be writing from a blog purgatory, where they knew they had to write an entry every week and they'd given up on anyone ever reading or caring about their work. Their blog entries read like bank statements. They were passionless, with no consideration for the reader. These types of blog entries are sad, uninteresting inner monologues that should remain inside the heads of the writers, unworthy to be called actual blogs.

Mike Volpe of HubSpot, an inbound marketing system that helps small to mid-sized businesses increase their online presence, suggests using social media as part of an overall inbound marketing strategy. He suggests pairing it with a blog or other informative media pieces like articles or videos. Over the years, Mike has learned to optimize his Web content for SEO (Search Engine Optimization), and to create interactive landing pages to engage visitors. "Because we use social media as part of our overall inbound marketing strategy, social media is one of our top five sources for leads and sales," says Mike. "We're a startup, but this strategy is a core part of how we have grown from twelve customers to over one thousand customers in the past two years." To date, Mike's blog has over 10,000 subscribers and is one of the top marketing blogs available. Mike works to keep his social media up-to-date, relevant, and easy to find.

Small business focused blogs come in all shapes and sizes, and rarely are any two alike. Some bloggers talk about their business selling free-trade coffee, while others review high-end cars and racing bikes.

While blog types vary, here are a few points to remember when writing a blog for your business:

- Keep your entries short. Generally, a blog entry is no more than a couple of paragraphs in length.
- Keep your entries focused. Find one subject and stick to it.
- Keep it consistent. Blog readers expect consistent content, so I suggest blogging anywhere from once a week to once a month. This way your readers keep coming back, and they generally know when you're going to add a new blog entry.
- Keep it personal. Blog entries are a "behind the scenes" look at your business. Find a way to let blog readers and potential customers see the inside of your business, without giving away trade secrets, and you will find a balance that is worth treading.

A blog is a very personal thing and, if you have one, I suggest keeping in mind the persona from which your blog is written. Is your company a snowboard manufacturer, that has an edgy, super-cool blog voice, designed to glamour teens into thrashing the slopes through a wave of pure white powder? Or, perhaps your organic wine company is looking for the Über-Neo-Foodie voice entrenched in pagan culture, and opposed to anything that may block the very karma that holds all life forces together. Regardless, write your blog for your audience and expect that it will be read.

Rule 8

People Recognize Bad Viral Behavior

Don't write a review of your own company, unless you know how.

One of the hallmarks of any good marketing campaign is honesty, or at least as much honesty as possible. Your social media efforts should follow the same philosophy. People recognize bad viral behavior. When you are dishonest in social media, it can be very obvious to others and potentially come back to harm your business.

Nothing says, "No one can see me. I'm invisible," like writing an online review for your own business. Your customers are smarter than that and when people find out you wrote your own review your social media reputation will suffer. It's the social equivalent of calling a friend, and telling them how awesome you are, while pretending to be someone else. In the business world it's unethical, and if you're found out, it doesn't look very good.

There are ways to ensure your online presence is well maintained without creating a false online personality and pretending to be someone else. Asking a friend to enter your company information on a wiki site like Wikipedia is acceptable, but pretending to be a customer and writing a review of your product is a social media taboo. Writing a good review for one of your affiliates and asking them to write a review of your business is also acceptable.

Here is a theoretical example of the difference between a real customer versus an employee reviewing a hotel.

Sunshine Hotel Employee (or Viral PR Person)

Sunshine Hotel is an exquisite location for any social occasion imaginable. My new husband and I just spent the week enjoying the luxurious California ambiance. The town features five star dining accommodations and great shopping. The Sunshine Hotel and staff treated us like royalty and booking our wedding reception there couldn't have been a better choice. Everything was splendid and many people commented on the plush décor, the succulent vegetation, and the amazing food prepared by the hotel's world famous Chef Alifante. The internet connectivity in every room was very useful for last minute preparations, and it was great to have free HBO and a fifty-inch plasma television to watch it on. My husband and I enjoyed the free limo service provided by Club Limoneto, and we plan to have our anniversaries there for years to come.

Actual Sunshine Hotel Customer

My kids loved the pool and my wife and I liked the gym. It was very clean and I'd go there again.

The telltale signs that a PR person wrote the first review are littered throughout the review. First of all, they used more adjectives than a normal reviewer would have without opening a thesaurus. Second, they repeat the name of the hotel throughout the review. A real customer isn't likely to say "Sunshine Hotel" because they expect that people already know what hotel they're talking about. In addition, a review from an actual customer would only include top-of-mind benefits like the pool or the gym. Unless the dining really was spectacular and they had time to write an extensive review, the average reviewer isn't going to remember that the hotel offers free HBO and high-speed internet in every room. They aren't going to remember the name of the hotel's chef, or the limousine service. In short, a normal reviewer will write a short review. They will be honest about what they like and dislike, and they will not try and up sell the company or product they are reviewing. They'll leave that to the professionals.

Rule 9

When 1 Person Complains, 100 Support You, And 500 Don't Even Notice

Keep that stiff upper lip. Just don't trip over it.

Online threads are fascinating to read. Many times, they are virtual arguments, frozen in time, for all to see, like the mosquito fossilized in amber, and discovered millions of years later. The context of the original mosquito, as well as the context of the original conversation, are both lost in time. Posts to online forums, or even feedback on a YouTube video often outweigh the very topics and media to which they refer. Having worked with businesses and their online personas, I've learned that business owners take comments left on their sites personally, as if the customer had walked into their store, and yelled their thoughts over a megaphone.

It has been my experience that people who have problems with a business are more likely to complain than those who have a positive experience. Don't take it too personally. If you are or know an avid eBay seller, they will most likely have very strong feelings about the negative feedbacks they receive. It's the equivalent of a scratch on a new car. The owner is the only person who usually notices. Now, if you have a gaping dent, and your bumper is falling off, you might want to seriously reconsider your business.

Jim Griffith, a.k.a. Griff from Rule 1, is an expert in helping eBay sellers and buyers use eBay effectively. "Embrace your concern about receiving negative feedback," says Griff. "Most people who leave negative feedback are buyers. They're not professionals. You, as a seller, are a professional. No matter what, you should always respond as politely and professionally as possible. State your case in your own words and try to make it good. Some people would just throw their hands up and say, 'The buyer is an idiot.' Of course this makes them look even worse."

When one person complains on your company's social media page, take it in stride. Consider its context and what the person is saying. If it is a legitimate complaint, contact the customer and do your best to repair the situation. Oftentimes, the customer will be reasonable and you'll be able to work out a solution to the problem. You might also find that successful resolution of the problem turns a "complainer" into a "fan."

If you've been an upstanding businessperson and adhered to good business practices, and you get a negative feedback or comment, chances are the rest of the people in your community who follow your social media presence will side with you. They know your business and your ethics, and they will understand that there are simply some people out there who enjoy complaining. If the complaint is recurring and illegitimate, like a hateful post on your YouTube video who is causing damage and inciting online quarrels, mark it as spam, or flag it to let the YouTube community know that your social media account is being unfairly targeted.

Often, if the complaint was a one-time event, hardly anyone will notice. While you should own up to any mistakes and investigate any legitimate complaints, it is not the end of the world if there is a complaint you cannot resolve. You are better off working to keep the customers who actually enjoy and respect your business and services, as opposed to chasing after the ones who can never be obtained or reconciled. While a negative feedback or comment can eat away at your subconscious, don't let it. It will sap your energy and leave you feeling alone and depressed about something that you should have handled and gotten over long ago. Move on with your business and your social media presence, knowing that you did your best to resolve the situation, and that most people will probably not even notice the complaint.

Rule 10

Not Everyone Follows The Rules

Understand the context of other people's online communication and improve the odds that you'll be a responsible member of your social media community.

Accidents happen in the realm of social media. Sometimes these events are intentional, and sometimes people who cause them aren't even aware they've done something wrong. People flag and delete media posts that really aren't inappropriate. People get into arguments and their worst sides come out. Quick-to-judge comments left on people's social media profiles are offensive and sometimes cruel. Since social media is a social platform that involves people, it is a lot like the break room at work, or a busy restaurant; people engage in dialogue with each other and often make the same mistakes online that they make in real life. They can say things out of turn, butt-in, and engage in communication that can be aggressive and rude.

When you are the target of these events it is easy to feel discouraged, angry, and even violated. If you've spent the last half hour writing the perfect craigslist post advertising your company's skills and services to the community, only to have it flagged for no apparent reason, you'll probably be upset. You may even give up on a particular social media community after a negative experience.

Sometimes simple misunderstandings can leave a scar on a business's online reputation. Throughout my career, I have met eBay sellers who can talk for hours about a negative experience with a buyer. Often, in these cases, a buyer accidentally leaves a negative feedback instead of a positive one. Sometimes they don't read the final terms of the sale and become upset when asked to pay shipping and handling. Unfortunately, these events can get out of control. What starts as a simple misunderstanding, sometimes escalates into a feud on eBay's blog, which involves many sellers, buyers, and bystanders.

So what can you do when someone in your social media space fails to follow the rules? Be ready and be aware. The more prepared you are for an unfortunate social media encounter, the more likely you are to walk away from it unscathed and better for it. Remember, you have the right to communicate through social media, and so does everybody else. You also have the right to your own privacy, and your own social media space, as does everybody else.

If someone in the social media space is targeting you and personally attacking your business, you have the right to flag their comment, or if you manage your own blog, remove it. Malicious online attacks are generally not accepted, and are quickly flagged or removed, in well-maintained communities. If your company's social media account is repeatedly targeted by the same group or individual, keep an offline record of who is making the attacks and when. Document the nature and the context of the offenses and when you have accumulated enough evidence that the offender has targeted your social media account, email your evidence to the social media platform's ombudsman or customer care center.

Sometimes things happen that are one-off occurrences. Job postings get sniped, flagged, and then removed by competitive companies often in the same business that you are. Comments can be left on blog entries that are critical and rude. Biased and offensive videos can be uploaded to a social media community. Remember, when these events happen, you don't have to get involved. While it may be tempting to write an angry response to a critical comment about your business's video, it is better to stop and think. What was the commenter trying to say? Were they really trying to attack your business, or were they simply pointing out that your camera work could have been better? Were they saying they didn't like your business, or simply that your product reminded them of your competitor's product? When you understand, or try to understand, the context and intent behind other people's online communication, you're taking the higher ground and improving the odds that you'll be a responsible, aware member of a social media community.

Rule 11

There's Always a Reason To Communicate

The virtue of virtual communication is that it helps you reach customers the moment they need you.

Procrastination is a great way to spend your time if you're rethinking your life. We've all procrastinated over what we should be doing, and gravitated to what we wanted to do. Perhaps you've put off checking the mail because you didn't want to receive any more bills, or maybe you've put off sending an email because you were too busy googling your business name to see what others had said about you.

Unfortunately, many people new to social media, and even some who aren't so new, get frustrated with it. A number of people I've met over the years are intimidated by creating a blog entry and as a result, never even attempt writing one. They imagine it as an impossible objective to achieve, as if bloggers were superheroes doing things mere mortals are incapable of doing. The more these people think about blogging, the less they want to do it and the more they find other things to do.

I suggest staying up-to-date with your social media not only because a stale blog is the equivalent of a presentation printed on a dot matrix printer, but because keeping up with social media forces us to stay current. When you post "What I'm working on now" on your Facebook or LinkedIn page, you're forcing yourself to think about what it is you're actually working on. These posts, however simple they may seem, force you to focus on the *now*, and hopefully by being in the now you can learn to continue doing what needs to be done and avoid procrastinating.

As a business, you have to be competitive, and if your competition hasn't discovered how to maximize your industry for social media yet, it's just a matter of time before they do.

Sky Khan, founder of Tedde, (http://www.tedde.com) an inventive teddy bear manufacturing company, has found success on both Facebook and YouTube platforms. One of the strategies Sky uses to increase awareness of Tedde in the social media space is to include a physical flyer and coupon in a customer's order, offering a discount on their next purchase if they fan Tedde's Facebook page. Sky's edgy and creative teddy bears and bear accessories are also featured in a series of YouTube videos. The videos are short and funny segments featuring The Invisible Bear vs. The Cat, a music video featuring a lost bear at Coney Island, and a short satirical recreation of the famous YouTube video, "Dramatic Chipmunk." The simple act of putting flyers in the products your company ships, directing customers to your social media page, can have a lasting impact on how your customers feel about your company's identity and brand.

Stay one step ahead of the game by learning how to use social media and keeping up with your blog posts, webcasts, and Tweets. Remember, your social media efforts don't have to be perfect, but they do need to be consistent. Think of your company's website as its life story. Your social media activities are your business's daily journal. Weekly or monthly journals are acceptable, just make sure your social media is current.

Staying active on social media and putting in the time can mean generating new clients, as well as blog posts. Long-time serial entrepreneur Hugh Simpson joined the community at youngentrepreneur.com to offer advice from his thirty-four years in business. He wanted to offer the same level of mentorship that he himself had been given years ago. Members of the community began privately messaging him and the results of those relationships led to Hugh, not only mentoring them, but becoming a business associate with them for an India-based Web design company and also a medical tourism marketing project. Social media can be rewarding for your company, so don't hesitate to put in the time and give of yourself. If you are diligent and follow the rules, your hard work should pay off.

Part II
Your Business's Identity

Learn the finer points of social media; how to differentiate your business, gain a following, and make it personal.

Part II: Your Business's Identity

Rule 12

Build a Great Profile

Your social media profile is your business's first impression. Make it count.

Whether your business is using YouTube, Flickr, Blogger, MySpace, Facebook, or PhotoBucket, you need to know how to create a good social media profile and maximize your business's online presence. Brian Solis, Principal of the Silicon Valley award-winning PR and New Media Agency FutureWorks, describes social media as "Your chance to share with the public why you are someone they should know and trust. You, and only you are responsible for connecting the dots between customers looking for direction and the solutions and services they need to make their lives easier and more efficient." This means the public needs to recognize you across the multiple social media spaces you inhabit.

The first step is to remain constant across the social media platforms you frequent. Make sure people visiting them know it's still you. Write out a brief description of your company and your services and save it as a text document. Then, when you join a new social media platform, you can copy and paste the appropriate parts of it into the "about me" section of your profile. A profile quickly tells other community members what your business is and why it is in a particular social media space. Be as detailed as possible in your business description and use it as an opportunity to explain some of the success your business has experienced. Your profile is the social media equivalent to your company's *about us* page, so it should contain the following key elements:

- Your Company's Name and Tagline
- What Your Company Does
- Your Company's History
- Your Company's Website URL
- What to Expect (from your Company's social media account)
- How to Contact You
- Additional Company Facts

Once you have answered these questions, and any others the social media platform requests, upload an avatar to show the world who your company is. An avatar is a picture of you or your company. If you truly are the force behind your company's social media campaign, and without you your company would no longer exist, use your own picture. Make sure the picture still looks like you when it's scaled down to an inch by an inch. Ideally, your picture will be a headshot, cropped at the shoulders or elbow, and taken against a relatively solid background. You want to stand out from the background, and you want your picture to be recognizable across all of your social media platforms.

Read profiles of other members of your social media community and look for users whom you find compelling.

- What have they done that is different from other members?
- What branding elements do they use to let you know they're a business?
- Why do you feel connected to their profile more than others?

"The more real you appear and act in the space the better the customers and market respond to you and the communication you put out," says Scott Bradley, the force behind the marketing campaign for Mike Michalowicz's book 'The Toilet Paper Entrepreneur.' Scott's effort in the social media space was not focused on garnering millions of friends, but instead on focused personally relatable product and brand identity.

"We engage our community by featuring guest posts by our readers, profiling other passionate followers, and producing high quality content that serves our market. We then use the social media channels to push out our message through social bookmarking sites," says Scott. "With my guidance, Mike has been able to build plenty of social capital to help him effectively serve his market in a way that is unique from any other author who is using the technology."

Because the rules of every social media platform are dependent on their community, take notes on the answers to these questions and learn as much as you can from them about how to grow your social media profile and maximize it for success.

Rule 13: Not Everyone Needs a MySpace Page

Unless you are your business, there are social media platforms out there that can meet your business needs more than a site designed for friends who want to network.

If you're reading this book, chances are you've heard of, or even used, MySpace. Founded in 2003, at the dawn of the social media era, MySpace is one of the most well known, and established social media platforms, and it is commonly top-of-mind when considering social media. Unfortunately, if you're new to social media, it is not one of the easiest platforms to use and, depending on your business's social media needs, MySpace may not be the right place for your business's social media page.

On the positive side, MySpace has over 100 million users around the globe. It can be a great place to advertise, and MySpace has detailed demographic information about its users. They know a user's gender, favorite book, age, location, occupation, education level, and what "mood" that person is in. They also know about a user's network, who their friends are, where they live, and what their relationship is. MySpace is a company that truly knows its audience and uses that to its advantage.

While building a MySpace profile for your company may sound like a dream come true, the reality is that your company may not be right for MySpace. According to their website, MySpace is "an online community that lets you meet your friend's friends." For companies looking to create a MySpace page for their entire company, this should be a red flag. A business is not an individual. MySpace is for actual individuals.

The list does not include businesses looking to increase product awareness, or companies promoting their brand, although many companies and businesses do just that. The point of social media is that you interact with customers and potential customers with open, honest communication that develops trust and eventually secures their business and repeat business. While it is perfectly acceptable to have your own personal MySpace page and connect with your friends in real life, it may not be appropriate for your business to promote its alter ego in a social media profile.

Having a MySpace profile to promote your business can work if you are an individual who happens to be their business, like a singer, or an artist. Many well-known musicians and indie musicians have a MySpace page and because MySpace was designed for individuals, this is a perfectly acceptable way to use the community. If you are such a person, with such a business, use your MySpace page to reinforce your image and connect with people. Know what your goals are. Are you there to make a lot of friends? Are you there to increase your online visibility? Are you there to let fans hear your music, or see your artwork? Keep your goals in mind and they will help define the look and feel of your MySpace page.

Different social media platforms have different benefits. If you want instant responses from a mass audience, MySpace probably isn't the platform for you. "I use Twitter because it's the fastest," says John Chow, founder of The TechZone. "Social media has been a big part of the growth of my blog and it offers a direct link to your customers. During the swearing in of President Obama, I sent out a tweet on Twitter asking, *The President lives in the White House. Where does the VP Live*? I got the answer in less than a minute from a dozen people." Remember, not everyone needs a MySpace page and unless you are your business, there are social media platforms out there that will meet your needs more than a site designed for friends who want to network.

Rule 14

Meet With Customers Virtually

It's easier to coordinate meetings and save travel expenses if you embrace the technology of webinars.

Remember the last time your small business went to an industry-related convention, seminar, or lecture? Unless it was held in your hometown, there was probably a great deal of travel, time, and energy involved on your part. While you may have had a little exposure for your business, these types of events may not be as cost-effective and impacting as they used to be, especially with the technology of webinars.

It's been my experience that webinars are the green alternative to traditional, in-person events. They're also a great way to reach your audience without inconveniencing attendees and their pocketbooks. BrightTalk CMO Jan McDaniel explains that people host webinars for a variety of reasons; they want a measurable marketing effort, and they have more to say than they can possibly communicate through traditional marketing tools. "They want to be on an even playing field with companies ten to one-hundred times their size," Jan says. "The reach is fantastic. You can watch your audience build over time and have an ongoing, engaged relationship with your viewers."

For small businesses who want to communicate once with their audience, for something like a one-time sales presentation, with no intention of ongoing virtual engagement with their audience, Jan suggests services like WebEx. However, if your small business wants to syndicate its webcast and reach a large audience, BrightTalk will better serve your needs. "Our small businesses have found webcasting works best when they are able to do it every six to eight weeks," says Jan. "They love to have more time to speak with their audience, and they feel it sets them apart from the competition."

While a singular webinar may not generate billions of online visitors, it should grab your target demographic and communicate your key messages. Give your customers a reason to tune in, and if you're doing multiple webinars, give them a reason to come back, by keeping your content upbeat, interesting, and appropriate to your business. Thoughtful social media generates thoughtful people, so spend time making your company's webinars havens of information and entertainment relevant to your business segment. Study what other companies are doing, watch their webinars and test what works and what doesn't.

PowerPoint can be a powerful tool in which to create your webinar, and because its relatively simple to use and inexpensive virtually any company can create a presentation that shows off the benefits of their services or products. Here are some pointers for creating an effective webinar:

- Layout your key points before you begin
- Write a script based on these key points
- Make sure each slide has the same header and/or footer (your name, the date, and your company's name)
- Use graphics that illustrate your point
- Don't fill each slide to the brim with text
- Practice and time your webinar

If possible, practice your webinar with a friend or business colleague and get their feedback. It's easy to assume that you've made a critical point, when in truth, you may have skipped it. A second opinion will help. It is also important to pay attention to the way your presentation looks. Do your graphics look consistent? Do they clearly illustrate what you are trying to say? Is there too much text in your slides? Remember, your webinar is a great way to establish yourself as an expert in your industry and establish a reputation a trusted brand. You don't have to buy a plane ticket and spend all day on your feet at a convention. You can give the presentation from your living room and no one will know the difference. In fact, they'll appreciate it.

Rule 15

Use Your Own Media

If you don't own the rights to it, don't use it.

Today, there are many online clip art libraries for businesses to use. Some of the clip art is free, some of it requires a monthly subscription, and some of it is pay-per-use. Look at just about any corporate website, sales presentation, and PowerPoint presentation and you'll find pictures that scream, "I came from a business clip art library!" These pictures commonly feature a professionally dressed businessperson sitting in front of a computer, smiling dreamily at the screen. Sometimes they feature a smiling business professional holding a large round red and white target. The subjects of these pictures are usually in a clean, well-lit environment that looks like the stereotypical image of every office around the world.

There is one problem with clip art; it doesn't show customers and potential customers your business. While purchased pictures may be pretty, they are only able to show people a concept of what your business does. They cannot show people what your office looks like, or what your CEO looks like, or what your employees actually do on a day-to-day basis.

While the temptation of using clip art on your social media page can be great, remember, social media is personal. People expect to see pictures, videos, sound clips, and stories that stem directly from your business and the people who run it. While composing a photo essay for your blog about your company's construction of your signature chocolate chip cookie might seem mundane to you, it can be fascinating to your customers and cookie connoisseurs worldwide. Do not underestimate your daily efforts. Publicize them across your social media pages, let people know that your cookie recipe was passed down from your great-grandmother who didn't tell anyone the secret ingredient until she was on her death bed. These details yield themselves to social media; they are interesting to your audience, and the very elements that keep your business going.

If you do not have a substantial library of pictures of your business, build one. Study traditional clip art, and then take your camera and shoot your own. Take close up pictures of the common elements of your business; your employees, your workspace, the front of the building if you have a brick and mortar facility, your products, and even the coffee cup on your desk. These pictures will come in handy when you're writing a blog entry a month from today, and you need a picture to go with it. Don't be afraid to take more pictures than you need; you can make your selections and edit them later.

Owning your own media is also a good practice to keep with your company's music and video usage. For example, if your business has created a YouTube video, be sure you own the rights to the music and images you are using. If you need a catchy song, and don't want to write your own, there are plenty of useable songs on websites like PodSafeAudio.com. Just be sure to credit the musician somewhere in your video.

Don't be afraid to use your own media and your own ideas. "Many traditional companies were concerned about protecting as much of their intellectual property as possible," says Daniel Scocco, creator of Daily Blog Tips, and founder of Online Profits. "Forget the old business principles and enter into the new game with an open mind. If you don't you may risk losing your market to a competitor who is more flexible and willing to share its resources and knowledge with clients and other players."

Rule 16: Have a Username That Reflects Your Business

The username that got you through college is no longer sufficient when you're trying to attract clients who will pay real money for your products or services.

Brand identity and consistency is an essential part of an effective social media campaign. As a business, you want to have a username that is consistent with who your company is. Your username can say a lot about you so it is important that you create one that your customers identify with, as well as one that is consistent across all of the social media platforms you use for your business.

We've all seen usernames that don't make sense or that don't work. For example, "yourbusinessname14." The problem with a username with a random number at the end is that it is confusing and it implies that there are 14 other businesses who registered with that social media community before you did. The same is true if you have a username like "yourname17" only now your customers are wondering why your business uses your name in its username. Unless you are an artist or a musician and you *are* your business, avoid using your actual name as your username.

"Use your business name, including an avatar, to brand yourself online," says Dan Schawbel, personal branding expert and author of 'Me 2.0.' "There are far too many people who don't take personal branding through social media seriously enough and they don't see the same benefits they could have." Unless you're a celebrity or a well-known business, known for your quirky handle, or unless your business is quirky and customers expect that from you, try creating a username that can be consistent across your social media efforts. Remember to keep your personal social media separate from your professional social media as much as possible. The username that got you through college is neither sufficient nor appropriate when you're trying to attract clients who will pay real money for your products or services.

In an ideal world, every business could have a username that is the same as their business name. Many times though, the exact username you want in a social media community is already taken and there is little you can do about it. When this happens, it is perfectly acceptable to shorten elements of your business's name to make an attractive username—just make sure it is recognizable. For example, since my business is called Jacobson Communication, I could shorten it to "jcommunication" or "jcom," as both of these names are easy to say and fairly recognizable. I would not, however, want to shorten it to "jacocommu" or "communicationjaco," as neither of these names sound like Jacobson Communication.

If you are unable to find a simple derivation of your company's name for your username, work on a name that resembles what your business does and choose a name that strongly conveys that idea. Once you have found a username that resembles your business and is recognizable to your customers stick with it. Make sure your email address matches it, and do your best to secure that username across various social media platforms, even if you think you may not use that platform. It's better to save it now, than find out someone else took your username once you decided to use that platform.

Rule 17

Build a Virtual Home

Turn your social media space into an industry force capable of generating significant interest and traffic.

Your social media page is your business's online venue to share a behind-the-scenes look at the people, ideas, activities, and facilities that make your company unique. Your social media page is a great way to improve your company's visibility and establish your brand identity. It should be interesting, fun, meaningful, and professional.

Visualize your company's social media page as your company's ideal break room. If money were no object, imagine what your break room would have. Would it have a gaming system in the corner, next to a seventy-inch TV? Would it have pictures of your employees of the month professionally framed and lit? Would it have a high-tech espresso machine with bags of free-trade coffee on the counter? Chances are, your ideal break room depends a lot on what your company's employees want and need. Your social media page is designed for your customers and potential customers; it should be built according to what they want and need.

Your social media page is a place that should be inviting to people who would like to do business with your company. Think about what they want. If you run a brick and mortar business where people need to visit your location to do business with you, add a map widget to your page. A map widget enables people to locate your business and customize driving directions based on their location. If your company is a business consultancy firm, use your social media page to share your client's success stories. If your business sells custom cakes use your social media page to show pictures of the cake-making process, and showcase your most recent work.

Your social media space is your company's virtual home and it should be a place where your customers feel welcome and catered to. Give them an incentive to come back to your social media page. Give them sneak peeks of upcoming products, interviews with your founder, and inside tips on how they can benefit from using your product or services. Discounts for social media "friends" are also a great way to quickly and cheaply generate return business. Your business's social media page should be a place your customers visit on their lunch break as well as their working hours because it is both fun and conducive to their needs.

A good social media page should be well-linked. It should link back to your website as well as be linked from your website. It should include links to your affiliate's websites, as well as prominent industry information. Linking to appropriate online locations enable your social media page to be an industry hub, where customers and potential customers can learn about what your business is, industry resources and allies, and the field in which you work. This will enable your social media page to be more than a place to share pictures and comments; it will turn it into an industry force capable of generating significant interest and traffic.

Glenn K. Garnes, of ConsumersWin.com, a website aimed at helping local merchants develop a higher Web presence via social media, knows the importance of building a virtual home. "We teach merchants, through our system, how to adopt a social media marketing strategy. We show them how to develop relationships with customers and stop viewing themselves as mere transactions," Glenn says. "We teach them how to use blogging, forums, instant messaging, online articles, and our internet radio show to communicate value to their customers and prospects. One of the more powerful things we recommend is to get customers talking via social media, about what they want, what they like and what they would like to see in the future. We teach our merchants to engage with their customers in a dialogue without expecting every encounter to result in a sale."

Rule 18

Get a Real Email Address

If you don't have a good reason for having your exact email address, it's time for a new email address.

Have you ever asked someone for their email address and after they gave it to you thought, "How in the world did they come up with that?" While the owner may think it's clever, in the business world the wrong email address can be the difference between people taking you seriously and sending your email to the trash folder. Would you respond to an email from *kittenstar74@emailhost.com* or *5zebrathon@unknownemailhost.com*? I wouldn't.

Because your email address is a critical part of many of your social media efforts, you should make sure the email address you use for your social media accounts reflects your business's identity. There are two major points to consider when choosing an email address that will establish you as a professional businessperson:

Email hosting provider: If your business's website hosting provider offers email addresses that match your business create an email address like:

First Initial, Last Name @ CompanyWebsite.com
(example: jjacobson@mywebsite.com)
First Name @ CompanyWebsite.com
(example: jennifer@mywebsite.com)
First Name, Last Initial @ CompanyWebsite.com
(example: jenniferj@mywebsite.com)

If your company does not have a hosting provider and you have to select your own, I recommend looking for one that you've heard of and that is likely to be around in the future. Using an email hosting provider that no one has heard of can be confusing to your customers and give the impression that you're not a professional businessperson.

Your username: The username is the part of the email before the @ symbol. While it may be fun to use your nickname or handle, it is far more professional to use a recognizable name. In some cases you might even want to create an email address for an entire department like sales@mywebsite.com.

If your username is already taken on the email hosting provider you want to use, try variations of your name or your company's name like:

- jennjacobson@emailhost.com
- jennj@emailhost.com
- jljacobson@emailhost.com
- smallbizsocialmedia@emailhost.com
- socialmediabook@emailhost.com

Having a professional-sounding email address helps potential customers and existing customers take you seriously and goes a long way to help you feel more like the working professional that you are. If you believe in your business and the services you offer, then believe in yourself and know that you are worthy of a professional sounding email address. Give yourself that long-awaited email promotion today!

Rule 19
Edit Your Media

Well thought out, to-the-point media means more than epic, unorganized, four-hour documentaries.

One of the benefits of social media is that it is instant; the moment you publish or upload something, the world can see it. One of the downsides to social media is that it is instant; if you make a mistake, and fail to edit it, the world can see it. While your business's website is well-edited, clean-looking, and professional, many professional social media pages are disorganized, sloppy, and fraught with mistakes in grammar and choice of media. So the immediate benefit of social media is also its immediate downfall.

The reason company websites are so often held to a higher standard is because the editor of the website is not usually the person who writes the copy, takes the pictures, chooses the clip art, and executes the overall look and feel of the site. One person however can create a social media page, in a few minutes, and this leaves little room for the editorial process to take place.

Remember, your business's online presence is a reflection of who your business is, and the quality of service and product it offers. Whether your business has a website, a YouTube account, a Flickr slideshow, or a blog, you are responsible for making sure your business is professional looking and well represented.

Text and Web Copy Editing

While it is perfectly acceptable to develop a voice for your business's social media persona, be sure this voice matches your brand identity. If you run a bustling coffee shop for java heads, the voice of your social media pages should reflect the free-trade, highly-caffeinated, global-sustainability attitude that your customers expect when they are actually in your shop, purchasing a double-vanilla latte. It is not, however appropriate to let your grammar and spelling slide into a social media cesspool. If you wouldn't use improper grammar to your customer's face when they're picking up their drink, don't do it on your company's social media page.

Picture Editing

A picture is worth a thousand words. What can easily be captured in a picture of your company's founder reading to a third-grade class expresses an idea more powerfully to customers and potential customers than a paragraph about your company's outreach to local schools. Make your company's pictures work for you; take a point-and-shoot camera with you to work, to corporate events, and trade shows. Be sure to edit your pictures, as no one likes to see ten pictures of the same thing over and over, and no one likes to try and decipher an underexposed picture.

Make your selections; look at the pictures your company took at a recent tradeshow. Save the most interesting pictures that tell the best stories in a file labeled "Trade_Show_Selects." Once you've made your selections, open them in your photo editing program and make the needed crops, color corrections, and fine tuning adjustments your pictures need. Save these pictures with your company's name in the file, for example, "CompanyName_Web_Summit_2009." This way your pictures should be easy to find in Web image searches.

Video Editing

While Web video is an extremely popular pastime, the best Web videos still convey a story. Make sure the video you post on your company's social media sites is interesting, story driven, and to the point. Long Web videos often lose their audiences, and videos that purely sell product without providing a reason or a story are often lost on their viewers. Edit out the parts of your video that are boring, and unless someone is talking directly to camera, try to keep no more than five seconds between cuts.

Part III
Understanding Social Media

Learn about the dynamics of social media, different social media platforms, how to evolve, and how to hone your skills.

Part III: Understanding Social Media

Rule 20: Know Your Social Media Platforms

You don't have to know all of them, just the right ones.

While it is not necessary to memorize and keep track of every new social media platform available, it is essential that you have a fundamental understanding of the types of social media platforms you can use for your business.

Social Networking

Audiences of the social networking sites vary from quilters, pet owners, teens, and tweens, to die-hard musicians, writers, and physicists. The MySpaces of the world where all the cool kids hang out, have evolved into sites like Facebook, LinkedIn, and Twitter. Today there are many hybrids where grownups can blog, connect with their colleagues, see pictures of what their friends had for lunch, and buy their buddies a "virtual beer."

The features and interactivity of these social networks change weekly. Your job is to establish yourself on a site that meets your needs while learning what that social network does well. Some sites have great community forums where people of a certain interest talk about their experiences and share what they know.

Blogging and Web Publishing Services

Use a blogging platform that makes it easy for your customers to find you. Some sites, like Facebook, require anyone viewing your site to have their own Facebook account, and nothing turns a customer off more than having to give Web companies their personal information to view a page. Find a service that you can easily use. Read the company's *about us* page. Make sure they are not one of the "fly by night" dotcoms that may be gone tomorrow, taking your hard-earned blog with them.

In-House and Independent Forums

Chances are you already have a company website and, if this is the case, your in-house Web guru should be able to add a "blog" section to your existing web page. If they are really good, they will be able to have a section where your customers can discuss their thoughts in an open forum. If you do not have an in-house forum, there are plenty of online forums already in existence that should be appropriate to your business's area of interest. Depending on the type of company you have, and your closeness with your customers, a forum can be a wonderful thing. Many of your die-hard-loyal customers may be thrilled to spend lots of time on your forum, answering questions for you and raving about your products and services. These types of fans are worth their weight in gold because they're writing for the "love of the sport" not because they are a paid viral marketer (but we'll get to that later).

Photo Sharing

Depending on they type of business you run, this may be a great option for you. Artists and comic book writers love this option because it gives their fans a place to rant and rave about their work, and it establishes them as a force to be reckoned with in their field. While a photo sharing service may not be suitable for businesses selling accounting services, they work well for businesses that sell specific, one-of-a-kind products.

Audio and Video Sharing

If your company has commercials that have aired on television, it might be worth it to digitize the tape and upload the footage to YouTube. You can then embed your YouTube video into your website for your customers to watch. Be sure to customize your video or audio sharing account with descriptions about your business, pictures, and other videos, when appropriate. YouTube has a good variety of community features, including the ability to subscribe to other people's video channels. Remember—only upload music and videos that you have the rights to.

Rule 21

Learn To Evolve With Technology

Social media efforts need to be flexible with changing technology, while remaining consistent with your core message.

Social media are tools that enable people to communicate, primarily via the internet. Traditional media, like radio, television, film, newspapers, and even books are considered "push media." This means that a gatekeeper, editor, producer, or organization decides on a topic or story, creates a specific media package and pushes that information to an audience. In today's world, mainstream media is owned by a small handful of mega-corporations, and while there appears to be a variety of topics, viewpoints, and stories available, the lack of diverse ownership leaves audiences with a limited selection of choices that does not represent the true diversity of society.

Enter the internet. After years of development, the internet has become a global network in which people communicate with each other, and information is shared across a variety of platforms. The internet allows people to openly share, without having to go through the traditional channels of editing and filtering. If you live in a country that protects your internet privacy you are one of the privileged world citizens who can explore a level of communication previously unknown to mankind.

Instant, and often portable, communication means that the internet is always evolving. For example, let's say you had a bad experience at a restaurant chain, and the headwaiter refused to listen to your complaint. You could write the owner an email, post a negative entry to an online restaurant review site, review the restaurant on Yelp, and instant message your newspaper's restaurant reviewer from your cell phone, before the meal ever ended. Not too long ago, this would have been unheard of. This form of "push media" means that you want to treat your customers well and tend to your online presence regularly. Set up a schedule and, depending on the type of business you run, post a blog entry or update your social networking page anywhere from weekly to monthly.

Temple of Poi Founder Isa Isaacs began her social media marketing efforts across various platforms but quickly found that, for her audience, LinkedIn connections and costly Yelp ads didn't work as well as testimonials and YouTube links. She changed her social media efforts appropriately to focus on what worked. Today, she posts links to her website through her YouTube video's descriptions. "I've gotten purchases and new clients through YouTube as well as increased visibility in the arts community," Isa says. "I've gotten class registrations through social media sites and the testimonials I receive on Yelp push clients over the top to register for courses."

It is important for your business to adapt because your social media efforts need to be flexible with changing technology, while remaining consistent with your core message. Websites and networking strategies that may have worked in the 1990's are no longer relevant to today's audience that expects instant reporting on everything from news to celebrity gossip. If you learn to tread this unique balance, your business will be well ahead of the game because it will be both consistent with your audience and something people can relate to on an ongoing basis.

Rule 22: Find Social Media Platforms That Work For You

Go where your audience is. Stay where you understand the technology.

Using social media platforms that meet your company's needs is the foundation of your social media efforts. Without a reliable, known, and easy-to-understand social media platform, you might as well be writing blog entries in a bottle and throwing them out to sea, and buying air time for your company's commercials on a show that nobody watches. There are some great social media platforms available today and, while the list grows longer all the time, it is possible to select a few social media platforms that will be both easy to use and easy for your customers to find.

The sheer volume of social media and social networking sites available today can be a bit overwhelming to new online communicators. Ask yourself a few questions about your business and keep the answers in mind when considering which social media platforms to use:

- What type of company do you have?
- Do you offer a product or a service?
- What do your customers like most about your business?
- What do you most need to improve on?
- Do you have a new business?
- Do you have a business that has lots of existing customers?
- What do you need to achieve from a social networking presence?

- Would your customers like to see pictures of your business's travels, products, or events?
- Is your product or service something that would be shown well in a video?

By knowing the answers to these questions, you'll have a better idea of what kind of social media you want to produce. Some businesses might produce a monthly YouTube video on crawdad fishing, while others show their mixed media artwork on Flickr. The more tech savvy businesses may even get into the elite ranks of the podcasters.

The important thing to remember is go where your audience is. Without your audience, there is no one to be social with. While you may have found a simple-to-use social media platform that you're excited about, it does no good if your customers have never heard of it. Get to know your customers social media habits. Ask them what social media platforms they use. Find out how often they update their blogs. Become "friends" with them on those social media platforms and build your network.

Regardless of what online communities you join, or even if you create your own, be sure to tell people who you are. Include your social media page links in your email signature, and in your company newsletter. Link to your social media pages from your website and tell customers where to find you.

Learn everything you can about other members of the social media communities that you can. Read other people's profiles, see what type of pictures they upload, and pay attention to the way they communicate. Make your business's social media page as interesting and professional as possible. Remember, if a social media platform is no longer working for you and your business, it's okay to leave it. Life is too short to spend time with social media platforms that either don't work or are too complicated.

Rule 23

Eighteen-Year-Olds Will Always Be Ahead Of You In Technology

They may have trouble stocking shelves at the grocery store, but they can Tweet and upload a YouTube video from their iPhone like their life depends on it.

You've heard it said that children are the future. I argue that they are the *now*. While they may not own homes or pay their own insurance, young people play a large role in social media conversations around the world. It's a known phenomenon that teens always know more about technology than their elders. Social media platforms undergo constant changes and, while no one person can keep up with every new platform or feature available, the people who stand the best chance of knowing the most about it, (aside from reporters whose job it is to know everything) are teenagers. Yes, teenagers, the unsung part of the labor force. They may have trouble staying focused and stocking the shelves at your local grocery store, but give them two minutes with an iPhone and they can update their Facebook page, Tweet their friends, and make a YouTube video like their life depended on it.

Ask them how they do it, or why, and expect a forlorn stare and a roll of the eyes. After all, if you have to ask, you're no longer cool. If you're no longer a young teenager, this can be particularly frustrating. After all, you're a respectable businessperson with experience and an education and you can't email a picture from your cell phone to save your life. It's okay. Teenagers will always be ahead in technology. Don't let it ruin your life or drag you down. After all, you have life experience. You know how to run a sales team, or how to manage the family restaurant.

When your high school senior comes home from soccer practice in tears about a virtual breakup with their prom date, it's no different than a breakup over the phone, in person, or a note sent via a mutual friend or enemy. By the time you've learned about your eighteen-year-old's problems, the news is probably already spread across their social media pages and you may well be the last to know. Also, don't be offended if your teen doesn't want to be your friend on Facebook. This is their space for their friends, and their conversations and having "mom" or "dad" listen in to their conversations at this age would just seem weird. Your teen grasps the value of social media at its core; the ability to connect with others.

There is a valuable lesson to learn in this; if your teenager can keep up with social media, while balancing school, homework, the complicated social strata of their friends, the latest movies and video games, teen fashion, and raging hormonal changes—so can you. Sure, they were born with a cell phone in hand and a Snapfish account, but you're a smart person with a lot of talent and ambition. Social media is designed for mere mortals. It just so happens that teens have an extra gene or two that helps them commune online. If you can find a way to harness that charisma and that power, you're well on your way to a social media page that will draw in potential customers and have them revolving around you like planets revolve around the sun.

Rule 24

Your Social Media Page Is Not Your Website

Websites are professional. Social media is promotional.

One of the problems many people new to social media have is that they see no difference between it and their website. Both are online, and both are designed to attract customers. While the high level goals of both are very similar, there are key differences that inform you on the best ways to take advantage of both social media and your website.

While your website is where your company shows the world its most professional side, your social media page is where you can show the world exactly what your business looks like on a day-to-day basis. Think of it like reality television. While we claim not to care what celebrities do every day, we watch them religiously when our favorite celebrity falls prey to the latest reality show.

The voyeuristic tendency in human consciousness is strong. We like watching people who don't know they're being watched on hidden camera shows. The desire for this type of reality stems from our desire to connect with others, and what better way to connect than to see other's mistakes and realize that we are all humans?

While it is not a good idea to display sensitive information about your company on the internet, your social media pages are expected to be a lot more real and interactive than your official website. Because social media is very personal in nature, people expect a higher level of transparency in your company's social media efforts, and if your company is unable to deliver what your customers want on the social media end, you're less likely to win their business. With so many companies online with social media these days, if you haven't learned social media yet, it's time you learn how to swim before your business begins to sink.

For some new businesses, a social media presence is a great way to introduce themselves to their audience before their official website is ever constructed or public. Gary Wimsett, Esq., Principal of Balefire Representation, is an attorney who used social media as a placeholder for his online presence while his new company's website was built. "Our *baby* representation company spun off our law firm less than two weeks ago. However, I'd been making contacts on LinkedIn and Facebook since October." Gary says. "The response has been phenomenal and we're excited about the potential for social media."

Gary who started as a business blogger in 2000 evolved with social media and eventually began using sites like Twitter, Facebook, and LinkedIn. While Gary has used other sites for social media, he suggests only letting people blog for your business who believe in the social media communities they are using. If that person isn't you, let someone else do it. "In the social media space, it is impossible to fake respect for the tools. If you think Facebook is childish or wasteful, don't use it. Put your social media campaign in the hands of a technophile or a junior staffer with a genuine love for the space. In my company, I'm that guy and that's what makes our efforts pay off. I've had three legitimate business meetings with people I've met through Facebook and/or LinkedIn. These meetings turn into clients and these clients turn into dollars. I love to communicate and meet new people, so I'd be involved either way. The fact is: it helps pay the bills."

Rule 25

Engage Customers First. Then Sell.

Reach out and Tweet someone.

Getting to know people online is a great way to increase the effectiveness of your business. Online, you have access to someone's blog, their social media pages, press stories about them, pictures, and a variety of searchable sources that aren't available in the face-to-face world. Making your business a hot topic of discussion in the social media world involves dedication, creativity, and honesty.

Remember, while your business or cause may seem like the most important thing to you, it isn't to your potential customers. You have to remember what it is about your business that originally drew you to it. Why did you choose to sell a particular product? Why should people care about your car repair shop? Chances are, your business supplies something that people need or does something that people care about. Find out what that is and use that to engage them. After all, they can't care about your business if they don't know how it relates to them and the things they already care about. Re-evaluate your approach to traditional business communication and make room for new ideas and ways to engage customers.

Recently, WunderMarx|PR, a public relations firm in Tustin, California, needed to create a fundraising campaign for one of their clients—Laura's House, a non-profit organization whose mission is to change social beliefs, attitudes, and behaviors that perpetuate domestic violence. In addition to sending emails to colleagues raising awareness about domestic violence, WunderMarx|PR blogged about the campaign and asked the supporters and stakeholders of the organization to update their status on Facebook and Twitter with the following messages:

Twitter:
Domestic Violence Aware. Month: Give $12.50 right now 2 Laura's House. Shelter a mom and her kids. Tell 9 friends. http://tinyurl.com/6zqgwj <http://tinyurl.com/6zqgwj>

Facebook/LinkedIn:
Donating to Domestic Violence Awareness Month: Give $12.50 right now 2 Laura's House. Shelter a mom and her kids. Tell 9 friends. http://tinyurl.com/6zqgwj

Before long the news spread beyond WunderMarx|PR's network and even beyond the Laura's House network. Cara Good, Co-Founder and CEO of WunderMarx|PR says, "The key with any social media campaign is to engage and educate first, without selling. When we seeded the community with information about Domestic Violence Awareness Month, demonstrated our value, then asked for support, we gained a lot more traction. That's a lesson learned for any campaign, non-profit or not."

Cara kept her messages short, knowing that sites like Twitter, LinkedIn, and Facebook lend themselves to succinct statements. The messaging worked. As a result of WunderMarx|PR's social media campaign, Laura's House raised a total of $10,000 in the month of October. They were even approached by TechBiz Connection, a professional organization, interested in becoming a sponsor. Two members of the local business community even expressed interest in volunteering at the committee or board level.

Today, Laura's House continues to use Facebook even after the campaign and has a fan site where people sign up for regular updates and learn about Laura's House's key accomplishment and activities. Think about what you want your social media to accomplish and make an active plan for meeting your goals. Once you remind people about an important issue or problem, and how it affects them and their community, they are invited to begin looking for the solution and you will be there, with the exact product or service they're looking for.

Rule 26
Have Enough Lifeboats To Save Your Blog

Make a backup of your blog and never let go.

Before you spend hundreds of hours typing clever, down-to-earth, soul-searching blog entries directly into your social media platform, consider this; a server is a physical device that can fail. A server is the computer where Web companies store the media that people like you put on your social media sites. Unlike offline computer documents, this information isn't being stored on your computer. While most Web companies do their best to use secure servers and ensure their customers' data is protected, it is still a good idea to have a backed up copy of your blog entries.

Check your lifeboats:

- Create a file on your computer and title it "blog" or "social media."
- Depending on how prolific a blogger you are, create subfolders for each year, and each month of the year.
- Write your blog entries in a text-based program like Microsoft Word, Text Edit, or iWork and save them in their appropriate files.
- Copy and paste the text directly into your social media blogging platform. (This is also a good way to store tags that you frequently use.)
- Back it up. A text document of your combined blog entries saved on your personal computer, or even a CD is your personal lifeboat in case the worst happens.

On the high seas of social media we may feel safe on our virtual ships, but don't be lulled into a false sense of security. Any number of things can happen that are beyond your control and if you do not have a backed up copy of your blog text, you'll lose that information that took you so long to write.

Reasons you might someday want to take your blog elsewhere:

- **Lost Cargo:** Though unlikely, it is possible that the servers storing your blog entries or account information become damaged or dysfunctional. In the event that this happens, you'll be glad you saved text-based documents of your blog entries elsewhere.
- **Piracy:** Your beloved social media company merges with or is purchased by another company that re-brands the ship and changes course. In order to survive, it is sometimes necessary for Web-based companies to sell out or merge with other companies. While this may be a positive step for them, it can sometimes be an unfortunate situation for the end user who feels left out and marginalized.
- **The Ship Sinks:** The company that owns your social media platform goes out of business. This isn't so uncommon in the dotcom world. No matter how big the company may be now, play it safe and keep those lifeboat backups just in case.
- **Mutiny:** One of your beloved blog entries that may have been a little too edgy for some readers has been flagged or removed by the community. In some cases, your entire account may be banned, sometimes for reasons that are justified, and sometimes for reasons that seem vague and unfair. Don't let your blog be at the disposal of others. Keep a copy.
- **Abandoned Ship:** Since you never know what the future will bring, it's just nice to have a backup plan. Who knows, some day you might want to turn your blog entries into a book.

Rule 27: Real Customers Are More Than Friends

Money talks. Make sure your social media is paying off.

While it is exciting to have five hundred or a thousand friends on your social media account, as a business, you have to be aware of the impact you are having, or not having, on increasing your customer base. Granted, not everyone who is a friend is a qualified potential customer. Some of them may know you personally, and have other reasons to connect to your business profile. You should however, be aware of those friends who are potential customers. Treat them well and follow up with them whenever possible.

Since social media enables mere mortals to have a virtual presence, if you know what you are doing, it is possible to attract people who will attract more people to your business. If you can get a celebrity or someone with a large following to use your products and even help promote them, the gravity of these people will eventually attract customers to your business—if nothing else, to see what all the fuss is about.

Billy D'Angelo, CEO of SubConscious Threads Clothing, had been using social media for years and began using MySpace to promote his company's urban clothing product line. He videotaped company shows and uploaded them, so hardcore fans could have instant access to their content. Eventually Billy discovered his business had over 2,000 friends and through his network, access to celebrity rapper 50 Cent, who agreed to don SubConscious apparel in his next movie and upcoming VH-1 series. By targeting his audience even more through urban music blogs and sites like NewMusicCartel.com and this50.com, Billy's website traffic increased by 250% and his sales increased by 400%. Through strategic implementation of brand messaging, social media saturation, and celebrity endorsements, Billy turned his online presence into sales that provided profit for his business.

"I can honestly say that our ability to spread the word about the brand and our products via social media has allowed my company to grow its brand awareness exponentially," Billy says. "We have made such great strides in effective marketing via social media, because our demographic is defined by the structure of the media outlet." Billy learned that the power of real friends is that they don't just accept your invitation to become a friend; they promote you and even help you; even when that means constructive criticism. "It's electronic word of mouth. Our brand, like most other small businesses in America, was very under capitalized at the onset. So, initially, we would produce garments that would get seemingly great responses in our local market of Staten Island. However, when we went to shows, our garments didn't pack the same punch. Now, because of the rapid expansion of social media, we can post samples of our upcoming projects on the social media and get instant feedback."

Billy's network now enables him to quickly and effectively upload a post and communicate with his audience. "Can send bullets, make posts, have banners, and be mentioned on over 15 high-traffic websites on any given day. Those 15 websites get close to 2 million hits a day and many times will have more than one impression or link back to our site."

Make your customers work for you and make sure your social media is paying off.

Part IV
Mastering Your Skills

Learn how to master your skills as a professional social media communicator. Find out how to get more out of social media and stand out from the competition.

Part IV: Mastering Your Skills

Rule 28: Be Findable

If you can't find yourself, no one else can.

If a blog is written in the ether and no one can find it, is it really any good to anyone? The answer is simply, "no." While you may spend hours on your company's blog or social media page, if it isn't findable, it might as well not exist.

While that may not seem like a fair assumption, consider why your company has a blog and social media presence in the first place; you want to attract clients and repeat business. If no one can find you online, you're better off putting fliers under windshield wipers and standing on the street corner with a sign featuring your company's logo.

There are simple ways to increase the likelihood of someone finding your business's social media page and they include tagging, linking, and keywords. (Linking is discussed further in the next rule).

- Tags are words you assign to a page that describe what you're blogging or writing about.
- Keywords are the words in your written posts that key search engines in on what you're actually writing about.
- Linking happens when another website or social media platform links to you, and also when you link to them.

I suggest tagging at every possible phase in the social media experience. When you upload a picture to your Facebook account from your cell phone, you have the option of tagging it. Be sure to use as many appropriate tags as possible. For example, if you run a mobile dog grooming service, and you upload a picture of one of your furry clients to your website, don't merely tag the picture with the name of the dog. Include the name of the town (or towns) you serve. Include words like dog grooming, dog bathing, puppy grooming, puppy bathing, dog washing, puppy washing, mobile grooming, mobile dog grooming, clean dog, and the name of your business.

Take a moment and type out a list of possible tags for your business, products, and services. Think creatively. If you run a laptop repair service company, don't just tag it with laptop repair. Include broken laptop, fix my laptop, laptop, laptop battery, laptop screen, broken screen, broken laptop screen, new laptop battery, new laptop screen, etc. Save the list of your business's tags as a text document. If you have multiple tag categories, flesh them out in the text document in sections, with one section for each specific product or service that also includes all of your company's regular tags. This way when you're tagging your social media posts, videos, and pictures you can copy and paste the tags directly into the tag field saving you time and ensuring the consistency of your tags.

Without tags, your social media presence and your business is much more difficult for customers to find. If you have a great picture uploaded to your Facebook account of an antique car you've remodeled, and it isn't tagged with the make, model, and year of the car, it won't come up when someone searches the internet for a picture of a 57 Chevy Bel Air. However, if you've done your homework, and tagged appropriately, you're well on your way to driving traffic to your site and making sales.

Rule 29
Flaunt It With a Podcast

Educate them and they will love you.

It's never too late to start educating customers about your business through social media, especially if you have a great company or product that customers need. Scott Whitney, CEO of PodWorx, Inc., began his adventures in podcasting relatively late in the game in August of 2006, (years behind some other podcasters). He heard about podcasting from Apple Computer's 2005 press release which said iTunes 4.7 would support podcasting. At the time he didn't know what podcasting was but he figured, if Apple Computer was supporting it, he should learn more.

Scott's initial goal was to establish himself as an expert in the four "P's" of podcasting: Plan, Produce, Publish, and Promote. Scott knew the goal of every podcast was either to entertain or educate the listener and that the listener must either make the podcaster money or motivate them to take action. His first podcast increased sales for his company's website by 23% and since, his own podcast has lead to speaking opportunities and additional revenue.

If your business has unique offerings that meet a need, let people know. Make it the headline. Identify the specific need your product or business fills and create your social media messaging around it. Social media is a very transparent medium. If you don't truly believe in your business, people will be able to tell. Sit down and ask yourself why you're in the business you're in. It may be because it's a family business, or because it's something you chose years ago. Seriously rethink how your business helps people today. How is it relevant? Why should people spend money on your products or services? Once you have found the answer, use it to shape your messaging both online and offline. Scott reminds us that people don't want to be sold to but everybody wants to buy, so it is important to entertain and educate, not pitch. Teaching is not selling. Properly teaching people how things work enables them to naturally gravitate to those who provided their education.

A podcast is a great way to engage your audience in an intimate way, and even though many hail the television as an invention that enhanced communication, the radio had a greater potential for closeness, in my opinion. In the radio, as in books, things can exist in the mind. You only need describe the smell of your bakery in the morning and the sounds of the coffee grinders grinding to take your customers virtually to your shop. They won't be put off if the front window is a little dusty, or if a hair on your head is behaving abnormally. They are completely at the mercy of your words and the audio environment your podcast creates. Think about it; when a fetus is developing in the womb, it can not see but at a certain point, it can hear. So in a sense, hearing is something we experienced long before we ever looked at someone's face. This is one of the reasons that listening to someone on a telephone is different than speaking with them in person. Podcasts can be used to speak directly to people, without using visuals to enhance or distract. Well written podcasts can be a powerful way to attract a loyal following of customers who feel connected to you on a level that is far more personal than one they may feel with the ten o'clock news caster.

Rule 30
Link Like There's No Tomorrow

A well-linked social media page can mean the difference between being at the top of a Web search, or not being there at all.

Today, we live in a world that is inundated with cross-marketing, pop-up ads, and corporate branding covering even the floor of our supermarkets. It is no longer possible to buy a box of cereal that solely represents one brand. Whether it's your local newspaper featuring stories from national syndicates or the billboards in your hometown that advertise companies whose business headquarters are thousands of miles away, the days of single branded products are over. Nowadays, if you're walking down a city street and see a mural on the wall, you expect to see a logo next to it, promoting the brand behind the idea. It seems that nothing is entirely removed from branding and cross promoting in the modern world.

In an effort to reclaim the advertisement-free "open spaces" of yesteryear, and to stand out from every company under the sun who's desperately trying to throw their product in people's faces, I suggest getting smart with your social media page and the way you link and are linked to. You don't have to be included in multi-million dollar ad campaigns and paste your company logo onto every possible business with your potential customers, but you do have to be smart. Let people find you where they are most likely to find you; in an internet search and on specific websites of businesses whom you choose to have link to you.

Creating a successful linking campaign is fairly simple.

- Identify local businesses, consultants, and customers you think would benefit from linking to you.
- Ask yourself, "Does this business compliment my own?" If you own a thriving donut shop where businesspeople come every morning on their way to work and one of your customers owns the drycleaners next door, this is a business that by nature of its customers and their habits, complements yours. It is likely that on the way to work, businesspeople will drop off their suits and pick them up the next day. This would benefit the drycleaners, and you should post links to their website on your social media pages under "Friends" or "Other Businesses You Might Like."
- You can then ask the drycleaners to link to your donut shop from their website or social media page. Offer them a discount if necessary. Their corporate clients are then more likely to visit your donut shop because your business is both physically close, and recommended by a business they already trust.
- Link to these complementary businesses and ask for a link back. However, I'm not merely suggesting the age old "our friends" tab at the top of your company's website.
- Be clever. Write a blog entry review about a complementary company and, in the text, include a visible link to their website.
- Be honest with your review, but remember, this is something your customers will see, so only pick companies you already approve of.
- Linking to like-minded businesses who complement your own and share your own customer base is a great way to build your alliance with community businesses, and increase the likelihood that customers will find your company's website.

Rule 31

Spoon Feed The Press

No one likes to be the first to write about something because no one wants to take a risk. Prove your business story with social media.

The days of advertising-only outreach campaigns are over, if they ever existed. Customers are too savvy, too smart, to fall for the old "Mikey likes it!" campaigns, and to some degree, this is because we know too much. We know how media is made. We have made media ourselves and we know that what happens on television and in the media is largely fabricated and hardly ever one hundred percent true. There's always a catch, and as savvy consumers, we're trained to look for that catch; to find a reason not to buy, or to wait for a better deal.

One of social media's greatest strengths is its instant ability to provide information to a mass audience at an inexpensive price point. In olden times, about thirty years ago, reporters researched their stories by looking facts up in books, calling sources on the phone, researching past articles, traveling to specific locations, and talking to people about the subjects they were researching. Nowadays, with the 24-hour news cycle, and internet news sources demanding instant reporting, reporters are often swamped with time to fill. They no longer have a daily paper to write for. They have deadlines throughout the day, and sometimes, more space than stories.

- **Make it easy for them.** Write the story about your business ahead of time, and use social media to substantiate your story. Include pictures, quotes, references, and everything that will make a reporter look at your social media page and say, "Ah, I can use this. My readers will like this."

- **Know why your story is good.** If you want to pitch your company's new product to a reporter at the local paper, be sure you've done your homework. Know your story ahead of time, and make sure it is clearly available across your social media platforms. You should clearly be able to communicate why your product is necessary and why people should care. You should also have pictures of your product available for download, as well as an accurate description of the product and the functions it performs. Include customer testimonials and tell the story of the product.
- **Think like a reporter.** Remember, they're under a great deal of stress. They hear several pitches a day, and they're under constant deadline pressure to produce the next great story. In today's market, they're often concerned about the possibility of downsizing and simply being let go. They don't want to write stories that are too out there. If a reporter goes out on a limb and writes about your company's new robotic dog that is safe, smart, and friendly only to have your company get hit with a major lawsuit the next week after one of your robot dogs blew a circuit, attacked a child, and caught fire, the reporter will probably regret giving your company's product such a good review.
- **Make it fresh, but not too fresh.** Remember, no one likes to be the first person to speak positively about a new product or company. Also remember, no reporter likes to cover a story that's already been done by every other media organization. This is where clever use of social media can give your company an edge. You can use your social media presence to gather and post positive quotes from industry experts and reviewers. This way, when a reporter visits your social media page, they'll know they're not the first to approve of your story, concept, product, or business. They'll know you're a legitimately good story because someone else already said so. They'll also be more likely to feel grateful that you pointed them to such a great story. You're not one of those fly-by-night companies. You've got a well-written blog, filled with interesting content that can provide useful background information for a reporter's story. Your social media page is their one-stop-shop for references, research, and the story that will hopefully go to print tomorrow.

Rule 32

Friends Don't Let Friends Pay Full Price

Give them a virtual discount.

When you receive a birthday coupon in the mail to your favorite restaurant, you feel special. It doesn't matter that you had to sign up for their birthday club. You suspend your disbelief and imagine that the restaurant really does know you and the date of your birth. Seeing your printed name on the coupon lets you know the message is personal and creates a personal connection between you and the company. You may even keep the coupon past its expiration date and forget to use it entirely, all the while, going to the restaurant every weekend. It doesn't matter to the restaurant if you use the coupon or not. They've already earned your loyalty.

The same is true of social media; people love to feel special, and they don't mind giving you their basic demographic information, as long as you use it to their advantage. Give them discounts. Make them feel special. Some directory companies like MerchantCircle enable you to create printable discount coupons and post them on your directory profile. When a potential customer searches the Web locally, for your type of business, they'll find your MerchantCircle directory page, which you've already personalized with a description and pictures, along with driving directions, your company's business, and the discount coupon you created. By offering a discount on a directory page, you increase the likelihood that customers will smoothly make the transition from your social media site, to your business's actual location, and after all, isn't that the point of your social media efforts?

When Dawn Del Russo, founder of Bella Dawn Boutique and Image Consultants began posting discounts for her customers on Twitter, LinkedIn, and Savorthesuccess.com, she began to see significant traffic hits at her website, belladawn.com. "I created an exclusive coupon for my Twitter followers who received 20% off their online purchase with a discount code," Dawn recalls. "As soon as I posted the code I began receiving online orders. The great thing about a code is you can see exactly where customers are coming from." By posting unique coupons to each social media community Dawn not only increased her odds of attracting customers looking for a discount, but enabled herself to know exactly where her audience came from. Dawn even acquired two new vendors from LinkedIn, where she had been posting new specials and events. "I believe every business needs to make social media a priority," says Dawn. "I recognize how important it is and I am currently looking to hire a specialist exclusively for online marketing and Web 2.0."

Remember, social media coupons don't have to be complicated, they just have to communicate their message and a value. Whether your business is advertising a 5% discount or a 35% discount, start testing coupons and find out what works for your business. While holidays are a great time to send out social media coupons, I suggest finding creative times of year to give them out. This will help you stand out from the competition. Search onlilne for interesting holidays that relate to your business and if those holidays don't exist, invent one or two. For example, if you're the owner of a coffee shop, declare a month during the "off season" the month to celebrate your top selling coffee drink, whatever that drink happens to be. Be sure to offer a 50% discount to people who are following you on Twitter, and your other social media accounts.

Rule 33

Get a Guru

When you can't find the answers to life's persistent questions…get a guru.

Social media is a large field and at times even the most Web-savvy people get confused and frustrated, so if you're staring at your computer screen, wondering what social media platform to join, or how to leave a comment on someone else's blog, you're not alone. Rather than wallow in self pity waiting for lightning to strike, why not call an expert? Think of it as a tutor, to help you learn a new subject.

Depending on your situation, finding your social media problem may be as simple as not knowing how to upload a photo to your Flickr account. Or perhaps you're wondering why only 17 people have seen your YouTube video while 274,899 people have seen one very similar posted by another user. Whatever the reason, when you don't know and can't seem to find the answer to a problem that's keeping you from moving forward, it's time to find a guru.

Who is a guru? For our purposes, a guru is someone who knows more about social media than you currently do. Depending on where you are in the social media sphere of learning, this may be your grandson, your niece, or even the neighbor kid down the street.

Social media experts are a growing population. They can be found online, next door, in the fancy office building downtown, and even in the news. A good place to start searching for your guru is often a community-posting site like Craigslist.org. Before you post your request however, decide exactly what you want from your guru. Draft your post ahead of time either on paper on in a word processing program. Write down what social media platform(s) you are using, and the specific problems you are having. Also write down your long-term objectives and the type of business you run. Tell them how many hours per week or month you anticipate needing their services, and the length of the contract. The more specific you are, the more likely you are to find someone who can actually help you get your social media efforts off the ground.

In the event that your guru is a young kid they may work for candy, trading cards, or money for a new iPod. You may also be their first official employer, so be ready to write a good reference for them if they prove helpful. Younger gurus may speak a language that you recognize as your own, yet remains foreign sounding. It's okay, this is just *youthspeak*. Don't nod your head and pretend to know their colloquialisms for the sake of looking hip. When you don't understand something your young guru is saying, whether it's a reference to your online handle, or social bookmarking, ask them to clarify what they mean. This not only shows that you are actively listening, but encourages them to objectively think about what they are saying. Take your guru seriously. Respect them, and you're likely to foster a healthy working relationship in which they can show you the ins and outs of social media first hand.

If your guru is a more senior individual or even a social media consultant, be sure they are qualified and that they are able to deliver the information you need in a way you can understand.

Be weary of would-be gurus who:

- Charge a hefty fee for no apparent reason
- Promise the moon and never deliver
- Have questionable business practices
- Don't have any social media presence themselves
- Treat you like you don't know what you're talking about

Social media consulting is just like any other job. Be sure you set out your objectives at the start and stay on schedule with your goals. Life is too short to spend working with people who aren't helpful to your cause.

Rule 34

Blog Your Best Blog

Write about what matters to you and your business.

There are times in a person's life where they remember exactly where they were and what they were doing, and they can put themselves there like it was yesterday. These events trigger flashbulb memories in the brain. Some of the most famous in American history could be the assassination of John F. Kennedy or the attacks on the World Trade Center. Sometimes flashbulb events are happy, like when your spouse proposed, or when your child was born. For others they can be as simple as the iPhone coming out.

Blog about what matters to you. Why? Because life is short. We're not alligators and we won't live for hundreds of years (without major advances in modern science). You just never know what will happen, so make the most out of every single day and for that matter, out of every single blog entry. You don't have to write the Great American Novel in each blog entry and sit with a box of tissue and a mug of tea, contemplating existence every time you post or update your social media page. But I do suggest taking yourself seriously, and really thinking about what you want to talk to people about. That's all a blog really is; talking to people.

A little planning goes a long way in social media, and there are easy steps that can make writing a blog entry as easy as writing a grocery list. It's okay if your children still have to reprogram your microwave clock when the power goes out; this is advice that you don't have to be a tech geek to understand. Remember, social media is "social," so your regular participation is key to engaging readers.

Tech Now's Scott Budman of NBC 11 has interviewed businesses across the Bay Area who have learned to harness the power of social media. "Social media enables businesses to build relationships with their customers by catering to their specific needs. I've spoken with the owner of a San Jose pizza place who used to get complaints from customers that they were never able to get a fresh, hot slice of pizza. So, the owner began using social media to tell people when pizza was fresh out of the oven, and now customers know exactly when to get their pizza."

Social media platforms aren't as complicated as they appear and people who frequent them are usually trying to find information and connect with others. You have to give them something to connect to. Take a piece of paper and write down why people should read your blog. Does it help them cope with interpersonal issues, does it teach them how to do their taxes? Be specific and direct—for example, "My blog is about buying and reselling antiques."

For example, if you were an antique dealer you would say, "I write it to help *antique buyers and sellers* learn how to *turn a profit* and understand *why antiques are valued differently in different contexts and at different times.*"

- **Use Visuals.** If you can upload a picture of what you're talking about in a blog entry, do it. A picture at the top of your blog entry draws readers in and gives them a mental visual of the concept you are discussing. If you don't have a picture on your computer that fits with your blog entry, create one, or purchase an inexpensive, royalty-free stock photo online.
- **Get creative.** If you write a blog about your business which involves raising dogs your target reader might type in "raising dogs" or they might try: puppies, dogs, dog behavior, bad dogs, dog training, family dog, dog rescue, puppy training, etc. Make a list of tags for your book and keep it handy. Whenever possible add tags to your blog, articles, pictures, and video. Depending on the site, you may be required to put a space, comma, or semicolon in between tags.

Rule 35
A Little Planning Goes a Long Way

Do your homework; it pays off.

New members of social media often wonder what the best way is to get started. Is it a good idea to ask a friend, read a book about a social media platform, or hire an agency to promote your business? Jay Aaron, now a social media consultant, joined Twitter, not knowing what it was. He gave himself six solid days to learn everything he could about the platform via an immersion learning method; he read every tweet, retweet, and profile he could, looking for connections between them. Within six days he grew an effective flock of Tweeters and became a substantial force to be reckoned with among his fellow tweeters. Jay also shares his advice via his website, blogs, and other social media platforms. The key, he says, is to be honest and genuine in your online communications. When you're in a new social media environment, take the time and learn the medium. Learn how people communicate in that medium. "In real life," he illustrates, "you wouldn't walk into a room full of strangers and begin talking. You would most likely go up to a group, listen to what they were saying, learn what was appropriate to talk about and how to talk about it, and then enter the conversation." When you're on a social media platform that is unfamiliar to you, take your time to get to know it. Don't make the beginner's mistake and start commenting, blogging, or making a fool of yourself. Listen, wait for an in, and then speak when appropriate. "What we learned about real life communication from our parents when we were five, we forget on Twitter, when we are 35."

Social media is different from other forms of communication used for business because it enables us to see immediate results. While it may take weeks to get a business proposal approved or a new recruit trained and hired, it only takes the click of a mouse to follow someone. When someone follows or recommends you on Twitter, there is no waiting for a secretary to forward you a message or send you a letter. It's live, and this is where people can make mistakes. Their instantaneous communications are made public, and live, to the world. Therefore, take the time to ensure you not only know how to communicate via a particular social media platform, but that you know what you are talking about.

Once you have a firm understanding of the social media platform you are using, take your time to build your profile and your reputation. Whenever you have five minutes, whether it's on your lunch break, or right before you go home for the day, take the time to update your social media accounts. Keep these efforts related to your business's daily activities, and keeping up with your social media will be easier. If you've just acquired a new client, connect with them on LinkedIn and Facebook accounts. If you've just created a great media kit for your company, upload the PDF to Scribd, or another social media sharing platform. If you're at a tradeshow, take pictures with your phone and upload them to your social media platform. (If you don't know how to do that, find out. You're going to need it.)

Once you've figured out how to use a social media platform, you'll be well ahead of the curve. Use this to your advantage. Look for potential customers. Draw them to you. Attract them to you by educating them, helping them, and showing them the value of your business. Put in the time and establish yourself on social media. Then reach out and attract the audience you deserve.

Rule 36: Publicize Your Company Events

Be your own promoter.

Because of the liberating nature of its communication technology, social media can be an effective way to generate buzz and publicity around your company. Online viewers tend to gravitate toward live-looking "up-to-the-minute" social media stories and in-depth reporting. Some of the best types of social media posts cover events.

Events are a great way to substantiate the real things that happen in your company. What makes an event worthy of a social media post? Here are some examples. Your company has an upcoming picnic. Plan ahead of time and bring your camera. Take pictures of people and their families playing games, cooking over the grill, talking, and having fun. Post these pictures on your company's Flickr account or create a music video with online royalty-free music and upload it to your social media video account.

Events can bring your local community together, and introduce people to you who might not normally know about your business. If you are having an event where the community is invited, be sure to publicize it. Craigslist's "community" section is a great place to list and invite people to your event. Yelp Local, City Search and super pages are also places to promote your business's events. Many local newspapers have online calendars where you can post upcoming events in your community. Be sure to read a few other community events before posting your own. Write your post ahead of time and make sure to include the title of the event, date, time, and location, and a short description. If possible, include a link to your company's website.

Theses events can be store openings, community picnics or performances sponsored by your business, employee of the month nominations, a new restaurant menu, a new VP of Finance, a company partnership, or even a behind-the-scenes look at this month's inventory. During the event take pictures and video to document the occasion. If it's an event where the general public is invited, hand out business cards with your company's social media links on it. If possible, go one step further and have a virtual raffle. Have guests email you with the subject "your company name contest" in the subject line. Choose the winner a couple days later, after you've added everyone to your mailing list, and announce them across your social media platforms. Of course, there should be some kind of prize associated with this, just choose something that is appropriate to your business.

When posting information about your event, be sure to include:

- Interesting descriptions
- Pictures
- Links
- Video *when appropriate*

Remember to only make these entries as long as they need to be. While you may have a great seven-page interview with your company's new CEO, only blog the good parts and the parts that people will be most interested to read.

After the event, be sure to write about it on your company's social media pages. Where you can, post pictures and video. It's okay to post several short entries about the same event. For example, if your company sponsored a carnival, have an entry on the dunking booth, and a different entry on the pie-eating contest.

After you've documented these events on your company's social media pages, remember to link to or embed them on your company's website. Depending on your company, your website may have various places for such social media posts. Some companies post them in their *about us* pages, while others post them under "news."

Rule 37

Make a Killer Virtual Portfolio

Use social media to stand out from the competition.

Before the discovery of the wheel, or fire, business was done very differently; when you showed perspective clients a portfolio, it was a hard copy. Yes, a hard copy. We called it paper. Paper and overhead slides were what most businesses used for visual communication. Paper was able to hold both words and pictures, and Venn diagrams with the occasional tag line. There was once a time when paper was even used for business cards, but paper had its limits. While it was, at first, fascinating to see colored charts and graphics scroll out of a laser jet printer, soon everyone was doing it and it became a mundane way of communicating visual ideas.

Today, virtual portfolios are a great way to quickly communicate your business's value to potential customers and clients. Virtual portfolios can be done through a variety of methods and in a variety of forms. PowerPoint presentations, and Keynote Presentations, can be uploaded to social media video platforms like YouTube and Blip.tv. If you run a photography business, you can upload your photo portfolio to Flickr and play them as a slideshow widget on your website. Musicians can upload their music to PodsafeAudio for media makers to use in advertisements and movies.

In the past, when potential clients wanted to know more about you, they would ask for references. Today, you can show off your references virtually. Establish yourself as an expert through social media by joining forums and answering questions from other members. Forums exist across a variety of industries on a variety of topics and they can be very general or very specific. Find a forum that has potential customers, where you feel comfortable as an expert, and start answering questions. For many this is possible, and simplest, on Twitter. Sites like HootSuite enable you to schedule tweets ahead of time, and release them later in the day, week, or month. Remember, don't over-tweet, but get involved in conversations; reply to relevant tweets, and make sure you're actively tweeting, or communicating on whatever platform you decide to use.

Robert Cooper, President and Strategic Director of PlusROI Online Marketing Inc., spends some of his downtime posting "answers" on LinkedIn. Robert discovered that he didn't have to post constantly to make an impact, and that people were actively interested in his business if he was able to first educate them. Within two weeks of posting on LinkedIn's "answers" Robert landed a $20,000 contract with a person he answered a question for. Finding a good forum platform with active members can also lead to publicity. An author for MarketingProfs happened to see Robert's "answers" and contacted him for an article that was written about one of his clients.

Social media portfolios can include blogs, pictures, videos, stories, case studies, forums, and even LinkedIn recommendations. Be sure your company's website has a page dedicated to social media, that includes links where people can find you on Facebook, Twitter, YouTube, and everywhere else you have an active social media presence. Make your virtual portfolio work for you and you'll be well ahead of the competition.

Rule 38

It's All Fun And Games Until They Find Out What You Did Last Summer

Keep your personal life personal, and your business life public.

Everyone makes mistakes and it's a part of human existence that isn't going to change any time soon. Unfortunately, when you make a mistake on social media, everyone following you has instant access to it. The good news, however is that you can quickly correct it and do your best to prevent future social media mistakes.

Social media marketing author, Shel Horowitz once made a social media mistake and sent something intended for an individual to an entire social media community. However, Shel learned from the mistake and moved on. "In a way, it was a blessing," Shel admits, "after that, I basically stopped gossiping, and that's a good thing."

Generating an effective online presence for your business is an essential part of the modern business outreach strategy. However if you are on LinkedIn, for example, and one of your employees is connected to you, and their blog is connected to their profile, and on their blog exists a possibly offensive blog post they wrote from their cell phone after a few too many margaritas, the original context of that conversation can quickly get out of hand. While sites like Twitter may resemble your AIM chats, they're very different for one reason; they are published. The world can see them. Published content is different from private communication and if you forget this in your social media efforts, you're likely to make mistakes that will reflect poorly on your business and your services.

That is why it is important to check your social media on a regular basis. Make sure you are representing the best parts of your business, and not extracurricular activities that take place on the weekend. Make sure you're your profiles, and communication is something your customers can and should be viewing. What kinds of comments are people leaving on your pages? Has a long and drawn out argument over one of your YouTube videos gotten out of hand? Did someone upload an offensive HTML badge to your MySpace page? Keep up with your social media. Make sure you are representing the best parts of your business, and not extracurricular activities that take place on the weekend. Ask yourself if what you are posting on your social media is something your viewers will find educational and/or entertaining; you want to have a balance of both. Then ask yourself if your social media material is appropriate to what your industry focuses on. If you're selling edgy themed t-shirts to college students for example, your overall messaging and social media efforts might be offensive in some circles, but not to your exact audience. If you're offending your audience, it's time to reconsider your messaging.

There may be times that something truly offensive is found on your social media page. If your page is hosting the offensive material, remove it as soon as possible. I'm not talking about the occasional questionable word. I'm talking about the kinds of things that can detour business and drive customers out the virtual door. Now, if you personally have strong viewpoints or opinions that could be offensive to your customers, it is probably best to keep those on your personal blog, where your friends and like-minded people can engage in thoughts that are socially controversial.

Remember, if you run a regular business, your social media page is not the place to challenge the norm and take on the man. If your business is, however, all about being controversial, then of course, do what works for you. Just make sure your business messaging is consistent across all of your outreach campaigns.

Rule 39

Kevin Bacon Is Your Friend

You too can meet celebrities, and even become one.

It has been said that there are six degrees of separation—that is, six people between you and anyone on the planet. Thanks to social media tools like LinkedIn, you can find out exactly how you are connected to virtually anyone and, if you're lucky, you're probably closer to some of them than you think.

Social media has enabled people to rewrite the rules of communication engagement. What used to require letters, faxes, emails, and phone calls can now be done with a quick message or invitation to connect over a social media platform. Use this to your best interest in your business efforts. If you want to be well connected in your business, make sure your social media accounts are well connected.

I'm not suggesting sending random friend invites to thousands of strangers. Start organically. Look at your address book and make a list of people you think you would like to connect with over social media. Think back to business colleagues, clients, customers, and even supervisors and managers from days gone by. Make an effort to locate these people on LinkedIn, Twitter, and MySpace, and if you know them on a personal level, Facebook.

If your business is looking for a specific celebrity or musician's endorsement for one of your products, look for their social networking pages. Be sure it isn't a fan site or someone posing as the person you are trying to contact. Once you have located a genuine celebrity, find out where they're active, and message them. Be sure to keep your messages short and to the point. This is not the best time to gush about what an incredibly huge fan you are, and how when you were fourteen you had every album they ever made, and lit candles under their poster every night. Be professional and approach them with the same respect and honesty that you would like to be treated with. Include your email address and links to your social media and websites. Often, by Google searching a celebrity's name, you can find out who their agent is and how to contact them. If one celebrity says no, or is not contactable, move on to the next; it's their loss.

There are plenty of film stars, bloggers, news anchors, authors, poets, and musicians that could help promote your business and just because your childhood idol is completely unreachable, doesn't mean you should give up. In the industry, there are "A List" celebrities and there are "B List" celebrities and the line in between the two is blurred. While you might think your product would be an overnight success if a major movie star promoted it, you're probably better off doing your homework and looking for a celebrity that is known by your specific clients. This person doesn't have to be famous to the world, just to your customers and potential customers.

Map out the celebrities, (at all levels) who you think would pair well with your business. If your business supports a cause or non-profit organization, be sure to include celebrities who are also interested in your cause. Look up these celebrities across various social media platforms. You may discover your accountant knows the musician you've been trying to contact. You may read a Tweet that tells you the actor you've been looking for will be in town next month. Social media is instant, and since people's plans change from day to day, it is a great way to find out just how close you are to Kevin Bacon.

Rule 40

Maximize Online Directories

If your business is not in the social online directory, maybe it doesn't exist.

There was once a time when every business that was any business had a prominent space in the phonebook. Companies paid for expensive, full-page ads advertising everything from pizza coupons to hair removal. Today however, customers are opening their phonebooks less and less thanks to online social directories like Yelp, MerchantCircle, CitySearch, and even map directories like Google Maps and Mapquest. While there are some die-hard fans of the phonebook, if your information isn't correct in prominent online directories, or if you don't have a good review listed, you're losing business.

Run a Web search for your business name and see what comes up (you may have to include your city and state in the search if there are other businesses with names similar to yours). You'll probably notice several social online directories that list your business. Click them and make sure your business information is up-to-date. If the directory includes a link to your website, make sure it works.

While every directory has its limits, some of them give you control of your business's account. Here are some ways to stand out from the competition on a directory:

- Upload two or three photos that showcase your company's products and location
- Include links to your company's social media pages

- Include seasonal discount coupons for products or services
- Upload a short and interesting promo video of your company
- Add a professional description of your business
- Link to complementary, nearby businesses and ask them to link to you

Take advantage of these online directories. Remember they often come up before your company's web page, or immediately after, and they provide useful information quickly—like driving directions, and contact information. Think of them not so much as a hindrance to people finding your company's website or social media site, but as a bridge to solidifying your relationship with them. If there is more than one source that provides accurate information about your business, this only reaffirms that your business is legitimate, established, and healthy.

Make sure you have written a good description of your business and the services you offer on your company's directory listing and that your contact information is up-to-date. The more you can do to personalize your directory listing and let customers know that you take an active part in your social media presence, the better your chances of attracting potential customers to your business.

Rule 41 — Advertise With Social Media

Short little ads go a long way when it comes to getting new customers.

You don't have to have millions of dollars to advertise on social media. You can tell customers what you're doing daily with Tweets and Facebook posts, but if you want to go a step further, you can create inexpensive advertisements that will show up on other social media community members' profiles. While the tools used by social media platforms undergo constant changes, there are some tips to remember when you're creating your advertisements.

Pick an Audience

By now, you should know who your audience is, so drill down and be specific about your audience. How old are they? If you have a brick and mortar business, select a specific location. What is their education level? What is their annual income? What kind of soda do they like? Make a list of the important characteristics of your target audience and be sure to select these features in the social media platform's advertisement creation tool.

Have a Clear Call to Action

Whether you want people to try your new brand of coffee or come to your art gallery, be specific about the action you want people to take. Don't use an advertisement to tell people the unique and intriguing history of your business. Keep it short and very specific. It's okay to advertise a variety of products or services your business offers, just don't do it all in the same advertisement. Pay attention to other ads in your space. Notice what looks good to you. Pay attention to what looks bad, or out of place. You don't need to reinvent the wheel when it comes to social media advertising; you just need to make it work for you.

Use Great Pictures

While many social media advertising platforms are text based, some of them allow you to add a picture. Make that picture count. Close ups work better than landscapes or pictures shot from a distance. Remember, the picture has to look good in an ad smaller than a business card. Choose a picture that illustrates the point you are making with your ad, but remember, it has to be eye catching. If you look at your picture and don't find it interesting, get another picture.

Monitor Your Results

Social media platforms like Facebook enable you to monitor your ad's results live. I suggest running multiple variations of the same ad and finding a technique that works. If your ad with the black and white picture gets 30 clicks in a day, while your ad with a color picture gets 3,000, start turning out more color ads. Don't be afraid to experiment with different types of ads. Just make sure you are communicating the right message to the right audience, and set your payment to something that you can afford. (You don't want to pay $1.00/click indefinitely. Have a kill date for your add campaign, incase you get busy and forget to turn it off).

Pay Per Click

While impressions are fun to watch, they don't equal potential customers and until someone clicks on your advertisement, it isn't any use to you. Pay for the clicks your advertisements receive. Don't pay for the many places it appears, but doesn't garner clicks.

Rule 42

These Are My Rules. What Are Yours?

Everyone has their own ideas. How will you get involved?

Now that you've mastered the rules of social media for business, it's time to go out into the world and do what works for you. If you find something that works for you, do it. Set your goals and don't let anything stand in your way, not even yourself. While social media is relatively new now, there will come a time, when communication evolves. Who knows what new avenues of communication will open fifty years from now?

As a citizen of the planet there are many experiences you have had that make you who you are. Your business experience continues to inform your decisions and hopefully the decisions of others. Isn't it time you shared your knowledge with the rest of the world? Well, of course you're going to be doing that through social media, but what about writing your own book?

"Write a book," you say. "But I can't write a book. I mean sure, I know everything there is to know about inside sales (or telecommuting, or closing deals with mega corporations, or the economy of green, or even mushroom farming) but I can't write a book. I don't have the time."

To this, I say, "You have all the time you need if you know where to find it." We all have other things we could be doing; checking our email, taking the kids to soccer, and filing those pesky TCP reports. However, I challenge you to think about what it is that you are really good at. What do you really enjoy? Is it worth writing about? If it is, consider writing a 42 Rules book proposal and sending it to the good folks at 42Rules.com.

While not everyone has time to write their life's memoirs, or an epic novel, we can make time to blog, share our stories and our business's stories on social media, and call our friends and family on the weekend. I argue that if you've come this far, you may just have the time to write your own book and, who knows, you just might help others learn more about the rules that make your work so successful.

Appendix

Resources And References

Resources

- http://www.blogher.org
- http://www.pnn.com
- http://www.mashable.com
- http://www.crowdscience.com
- http://www.merchantcircle.com
- http://www.ebay.com
- http://www.twitter.com
- http://www.helpareporter.com

References

1. Quote: Patrick Walker: http://tinyurl.com/ksozvg as seen on 2.28.2009.
2. Quote: Phillip K. Dick: http://tinyurl.com/npccdk as seen on 2.28.2009.
3. About Chris Hughes: http://tinyurl.com/6jek93 as seen on 2.28.2009.
4. Chris Hughes - November 7, 2008 at 5:23 pm EST: http://tinyurl.com/6xv8xu as seen on 2.28.2009.

Tool Kit

Apply what you've learned and jump-start your business's social media success today with a '42 Rules of Social Media for Small Business' Tool Kit. To learn more visit: http://42rules.com/social_media_for_small_business.

About the Author

Jennifer L. Jacobson is a communicator specializing in Public Relations, Brand Identity, and Strategic Sales. As a Public Relations Professional, Jennifer creates powerful campaigns that have had her clients featured on Oprah and Friends, DisneyFamily.com, The Huffington Post, and The American Marketing Association's Marketing News. Jennifer's brand identity services have shaped company and product images for Retrevo, LookSmart Ltd., Merchant Circle, Impact Marketing, MarketCulture, and The Personal News Network. As a strategic sales professional, Jennifer has the unique ability to grow a sales campaign from the ground up and turn cold leads into clients almost overnight. Jennifer enjoys identifying and forging relationships with key decision makers from independent businesses to Fortune 500 companies.

As the Founder of Jacobson Communication, Jennifer guides strategic outreach campaigns and growing companies. Jennifer holds a Master's Degree in Broadcast Communications from San Francisco State University and has produced commercials, webinars, podcasts, blogs, social media campaigns, and web pages for many of her clients. To learn more visit http://www.JacobsonCommunication.com.

Your Rules

Write Your Own Rules

You can write your own 42 Rules book, and we can help you do it—from initial concept, to writing and editing, to publishing and marketing. If you have a great idea for a 42 Rules book, then we want to hear from you.

As you know, the books in the 42 Rules series are practical guidebooks that focus on a single topic. The books are written in an easy-to-read format that condenses the fundamental elements of the topic into 42 Rules. They use realistic examples to make their point and are fun to read.

Two Kinds of 42 Rules Books

42 Rules books are published in two formats: the single-author book and the contributed-author book. The single-author book is a traditional book written by one author. The contributed-author book (like '42 Rules for Working Moms') is a compilation of Rules, each written by a different contributor, which support the main topic. If you want to be the sole author of a book or one of its contributors, we can help you succeed!

42 Rules Program

A lot of people would like to write a book, but only a few actually do. Finding a publisher, and distributing and marketing the book are challenges that prevent even the most ambitious of authors to ever get started.

At 42 Rules, we help you focus on and be successful in the writing of your book. Our program concentrates on the following tasks so you don't have to.

- **Publishing:** You receive expert advice and guidance from the Executive Editor, copy editors, technical editors, and cover and layout designers to help you create your book.
- **Distribution:** We distribute your book through the major book distribution channels, like Baker and Taylor and Ingram, Amazon.com, Barnes and Noble, Borders Books, etc.
- **Marketing:** 42 Rules has a full-service marketing program that includes a customized Web page for you and your book, email registrations and campaigns, blogs, webcasts, media kits and more.

Whether you are writing a single-authored book or a contributed-author book, you will receive editorial support from 42 Rules Executive Editor, Laura Lowell, author of '42 Rules of Marketing,' which was rated Top 5 in Business Humor and Top 25 in Business Marketing on Amazon.com (December 2007), and author and Executive Editor of '42 Rules for Working Moms.'

Accepting Submissions

If you want to be a successful author, we'll provide you the tools to help make it happen. Start today by answering the following questions and visit our website at http://superstarpress.com/ for more information on submitting your 42 Rules book idea.

Super Star Press is now accepting submissions for books in the 42 Rules book series. For more information, email info@superstarpress.com or call 408-257-3000.

Books

Other Happy About Books

42 Rules of Marketing

Compilation of ideas, theories, and practical approaches to marketing challenges that marketers know they should do, but don't always have the time or patience to do.

Paperback:$19.95
eBook:$11.95

42 Rules™ for Driving Success with Books

This book will help you appreciate the ease of creation and the depth of value a book (or series of books) can create for your business. Whether the author writes the book themselves, had their clients/partners provide content, or had it ghostwritten, you will be informed and inspired by the stories and lessons of others' successes with books.

Paperback:$19.95
eBook:$14.95

42 Rules™ for 24-Hour Success on LinkedIn

This is a user-friendly guidebook designed to help you leverage the power of LinkedIn to build visibility, make connections and support your brand. There is a theory that everyone in the world is connected by no more than 6 people. You know who you are, but who else in this socially-networked world knows you?

Paperback:$19.95
eBook:$14.95

I've Got a Domain Name—Now What???

This book is your guide to the many technology tools that can be utilized to build your web presence. Stages from registering a domain name to creating a website and utilizing your domain for email and internet marketing are outlined.

Paperback:$19.95
eBook:$14.95

Purchase these books at Happy About
http://happyabout.info/
or at other online and physical bookstores.

A Message From Super Star Press™

Thank you for your purchase of this 42 Rules Series book. It is available online at: http://www.42rules.com/social_media_for_small_business/ or at other online and physical bookstores. To learn more about contributing to books in the 42 Rules series, check out http://superstarpress.com.

Please contact us for quantity discounts at sales@superstarpress.com.

If you want to be informed by email of upcoming books, please email bookupdate@superstarpress.com.

Breinigsville, PA USA
03 February 2010
231846BV00004B/71/P